PARENTING SKILLS:
TRAINER'S MANUAL
Second Edition

RICHARD R. ABIDIN, Ed.D.
UNIVERSITY OF VIRGINIA

HUMAN SCIENCES PRESS, INC.
72 Fifth Avenue   3 Henrietta Street
NEW YORK, NY 10011 ● LONDON, WC2E 8LU

123456789   987654321

Library of Congress Cataloging in Publication Data

Abidin, Richard R.
    Parenting skills.

    1. Parenting—Study and teaching—United States.
I. Title.
HQ755.8.A2   1981   649'.1'07   81-13314
ISBN 0-89885-117-3-Manual   AACR2
        0-89885-118-1-Workbook
        0-89885-119-X-Set

TABLE OF CONTENTS

---

* Needs special materials.

PREFACE

For many centuries men of different nationalities, races, and religious backgrounds have struggled to obtain a "good life" for themselves and their children. They have developed and applied scientific technology to conquer diseases, to mass produce goods, and to travel in outer space. These scientific achievements have taken place largely because of the recognition of the importance of education and training in developing the skills necessary to achieve these technological goals. Yet, in one area, and one which is possibly the most important human activity, the raising of children, we have failed to recognize and plan for the development of the knowledge and skills necessary to achieve our goals.

It has been frequently observed by professionals and others interested in children that one must be licensed to be a plumber or a truck driver, while no requirements beyond the biological necessities exist for parenthood. The licensing of parents is obviously absurd, but this does not mean that nothing can be done. The question might be raised as to why so little has been done concerning child rearing knowledge and skills. The answers, undoubtedly, would be many and varied. The notions of mothering instinct, fear of domination by forces external to the family, the wide range of differing cultures and values are but some of the important factors. Further, professionals concerned with children have contributed to the problem by each suggesting the "right way." Each of these "right ways" starts from a specific set of assumptions and values and proceeds to describe how children should develop and how they should be managed. The failure to date of these efforts to be useful to the average parent is probably based on the failure to separate the technology of child rearing from the assumptions and values that underlie the theories proposed by the professionals. In addition, the failure to develop in the parent specific knowledge and skills has limited the usefullness of many ideas.

For years therapists have recognized that the unhappy, maladjusted, and unproductive human being is generally that individual who sees himself as having limited choices and means of achieving his personal goals. Effective intervention takes place when the individual develops the knowledge and skills to achieve his goals or is helped to clarify or change his goals so that they are achievable. In many ways the position of the parent is such that he has only a limited range of knowledge and skills applicable to child rearing.

Child psychologists and other workers often report that they have never met a parent who purposely reared a child to be unhappy, maladjusted, and ineffective, yet millions of these children exist today. In the course of clinical interactions with these families, what emerges are parents who are ignorant about their own values and assumptions and about the many different means of managing and develping desirable and effective behavior in their children. All too often serious problems in personal and social adjustment in children are related to gross knowledge and skill deficiencies in the parents. Poverty and physical limitations are important factors, but we know that the child is a sturdy organism who can cope with the conditions of poverty and physical limitations if reared effectively. We also know that children reared in affluence without physical handicaps can be unhappy, maladjusted, and unproductive when raised by ignorant and unskilled parents. What is needed, in part, at the present time is some means of increasing the chances for parents to develop a range of specific skills in child rearing. How this is to be achieved is not clear and undoubtedly there will be many different possible solutions. What is clear is that it is time to begin organizing the available knowledge and skills into programs of education and training.

The following set of Parenting Skills Sessions were created in the belief that many parents can be helped in the serious task of raising their children if some of the basic skills and knowledge required are identified and specified, and if the parents have the opportunity to learn and practice these skills. The author embarked on this task in the hope of being an interface between the accumulated knowledge of the various professions concerned with children and their development, and began with the professional literature, talks with parents, and personal interviews with about fifty leading authorities on children in the United States, in addition to his own clinical experiences.

The ideas and skills in this program do not represent the "right way to raise children"; rather, the program attempts to provide parents with insight and skills that will help them reach their goals. The ideas and skills are presented with a deep respect for the integrity of the family and the ideas and goals of parents. Each parent should feel free to accept, reject, or selectively use any of the skills presented.

HOW TO USE THE PARENTING SKILLS PROGRAM

The Parenting Skills Program may be employed by a wide range of professionals who work with parents and children. The only major skill required of the trainer is a democratic group leadership style combined with a genuine capacity to communicate acceptance and respect for the honest, if not always constructive, efforts of parents to raise their children to be happy and effective people.

The units presented in this program represent an amalgamation of a wide range of educational strategies and theoretical orientations; among those heavily represented are client-centered humanistic psychology, rational emotive psychology, and behavioral psychology. Each session or group of sessions presents skills that are effective in managing and changing behaviors of adults and children. No set of strategies is seen as being more important than another, and all must be employed with honesty and respect for others, be they planned for adults or children. Parents must be helped to see that the skills contained in this program are best employed in an open fashion. If their children note changes in their reactions and behaviors, then an honest explanation should be encouraged.

The program does not attempt to present a totally new method or rationale with regard to parenting or child management. Rather it represents an effort at drawing together the common knowledge and scientific knowledge available in the behavioral sciences. In designing this program there were a number of basic assumptions which were made concerning how the program would be designed and the mental attitude which seemed most appropriate on the part of the trainer towards the parents. To begin we assume that there is no right way, no orthodoxy with regard to how to raise children and further we assume that of all the various schools of psychology, and techniques none provided the total answer. The reader will find therefore throughout the program a variety of psychological concepts drawn from different schools of psychology, many which may appear at first to be contradictory, yet we believe that these seeming contradictions resolve themselves when the Parenting Skills trainer holds certain attitudes towards both the parents and his efforts. Number one among the positive attitudes which the trainer must hold is the belief that regardless of what parents currently are doing with their children, that they are putting forth their current best efforts. That is to say they are attempting to raise their children in a way which they believe will help their children to be happy and productive people. Further, we believe that the trainer must hold the understanding that the difference between successful parents and those who are less successful is often in a matter of the frequency or intensity with which any given parenting skill is used. We find so often that the successful parent employs many of the same techniques that the unsuccessful parent does. The most essential ingredient in conducting parent workshops is an attitude which the trainer must hold. He must have a genuine respect for parents, and this respect must be reflected in his nondefensive reaction to parents when they directly challenge either the content of the program or the methods of intervention being proposed by the trainer. A democratic leadership style within the group tends to facilitate the parents acquisition of the skills being taught.

STRUCTURE OF THE TRAINING SESSIONS. In utilizing the materials presented in each of the workshops, it is necessary that approximately 1½ to 2 hours be available for each training session. Each session is composed of three major parts:

1. The review and sharing of the previous week's home practice (20-30 minutes).
2. The teaching of the new lesson (40 minutes).

3. The discussion of the meaning of the ideas presented to each parent (20-30 minutes).

THE REVIEW OF HOME PRACTICE.   The review and sharing of the previous week's home practice represents an essential means of feedback between the trainer and the parents. This is an opportunity to check to see that you have communicated and that the parents understand what you have communicated. The second major role of the review portion of the session is to ensure that each parent sees the others trying the ideas and, at times, being frustrated. This experience of sharing feelings has a strong impact in motivating the parents. Different parents are naturally affected differently; some work harder because of the challenge and encouragement while others seem to work harder based on what appears to be a competitive motive: "If she can do it for her child, I can do it even better." Regardless of the reason, it has been our experience that failure to attend to the home practice results in a relatively passive parental response to the whole session, and ultimately, to the entire program.

THE NEW LESSON.   The structure provided in each lesson will assist the trainer in his initial efforts at running the program. We have found that with time, each trainer becomes less dependent upon the specific wording prescribed for a particular workshop and embellishes the workshop with his own style. This flexibility is encouraged as long as the objectives for each session are achieved. A straight lecture style has generally proven to have depressing effect upon the degree of parental involvement in the group; the group process tends to become highly leader oriented, and parental motivation to react and inject spontaneous comments is minimized. We have seen some group trainers use a lecture style to cover the content of the session, but this was generally achieved by making the main points and holding the lecture to 15 minutes. The supplemental points or issues were then brought out in the extended discussion period.

The most common style for covering the specific content of the workshop is the basis of the program and includes questions addressed to the parents about what was said to their children and how the children reacted. For this part of the program the trainer should be maximally responsive to nonverbal cues of noncomprehension and negative or positive reactions from the parents. It is not at all uncommon for the trainer to stop what he is saying with comments like:

> **"I think there are a few of us who don't like the sound of the things they are hearing," or "I get the feeling that some of you may not be getting what I am saying because of the way I am presenting it. Could you help me with some questions?"**

These kinds of comments are essential to ensure comprehension and to maintain a mutually respectful relationship between trainer and parents, which is essential for an effective program.

DISCUSSION.   This phase of the program demands the greatest degree of skill and empathy on the part of the trainer. The task is to help the parents relate what has been said during the lesson to their individual situations. Comprehension of the material may be weak and, therefore, parents may feel that the risk of appearing foolish is high. Candor and honest efforts should be recognized. The absense of judgmental framework on the part of the trainer is a must. This is the trainer's time to use reflective listening, to recognize the parents feelings as well as their words. During this phase, the trainer points out to the parent or group their own struggle with the ideas. The trainer does not tell them: "That's right"; "No, you wouldn't want to do that because..."

The trainer should respond to legitimate requests for information, but not to parental requests for judgments of their efforts, or proposed plans of action. This is a particularly difficult aspect of the trainer' role. The temptation to judge, particularly when the parent has done a good job, is so great that it occurs from time to time even with the best trainers. The fact that the trainer does not judge leaves the responsibility for the parental actions squarely where it belongs — with the parents.

BASIC COURSE (19 SESSIONS)

If the trainer intends to teach the basic program which is composed of the first nineteen sessions, he will notice that the skills taught in each preceding module and section of the program are useful in the succeeding sessions. The fact that the lessons are presented separately does not mean that the ideas and skills are not interrelated and complementary in nature. Parents should be encouraged to see how communication skills and relationship building skills taught in the first eight sessions relate to the behavior modification principles taught in Sessions 11 through 15 and to the Managing Your Feelings Sessions, Nos. 16-19.

SHORT COURSE NO. 1 (7 SESSIONS)

Objectives

1. To sensitize parents to the impact of their behavior on their child's self concept.
2. To provide parents with a set of skills that will aid them in managing their feelings in relation to their children and their spouses.

Units to be presented: 1, 2, 3, 16, 17, 18, 19.

SHORT COURSE NO. 2 (10 SESSIONS)

Objectives

1. To sensitize parents to the impact of their behavior on their child's self concept.
2. To provide parents with the means to evaluate their relationship with their child.
3. To provide parents with the skills needed to build and develop a positive relationship with their child.
4. To provide parents with skills to identify problem ownership and conflict resolution.
5. To provide parents with a conceptual framework to understand discipline and to guide their disciplinary actions.

Units to be presented: 1, 2, 3, 4, 5, 6, 7, 8, 9, 10.

SHORT COURSE NO. 3 (10 SESSIONS)

Objectives

1. To sensitize parents to the impact of their behavior on their child's self concept.
2. To alert parents to the effects of varying forms of discipline.
3. To teach parents the skills required to successfully employ the principles of behavior modification.

Units to be presented: 1, 2, 3, 9, 10, 11, 12, 13, 14, 15.

Special Lectures and One Session Workshops

In addition to the short courses described above, the professional using this manual will find that a number of the units may be used as lectures for one-meeting presentations to the public. The units suitable for single-lecture presentations are 2, 3, 9, 13, 20, 21, 22.

2. I am Worthwhile — I am Lovable
3. I am Competent — I am Responsible
9. Discipline
20. Developing Your Child's Intelligence: The Years Before School
21. Special Education
22. Helping your Child with High School Work

FIRST SESSION:
BUILDING A GROUP IDENTITY BY SHARING

The first session of your parent education program undoubtedly will involve some basic administrative matters. However, this session is the "ice breaker," and it is important that in some sense a group identity be formed. During the coming weeks these parents will be struggling together to learn and to practice some important child rearing skills. The more each member of the group feels accepted, secure, and unthreatened, the greater the chances are that he will try to tailor and apply the techniques and ideas discussed to his own situation.

During this session and the following two, the idea of group identity, and the acceptance, security, and degree of threat experienced by each parent must be uppermost in the mind of the trainer. The trainer must communicate basic acceptance to each and every parent, for it is the trust and confidence in the trainer that will, in part, determine whether the parents will be open to the ideas presented and will work at the skills taught. It has been the experience of the author that parents do not engage in behavior that they know will hurt their child. When these destructive behavior patterns seem to occur, it is because the parent does not see or know of an alternative way of handling the situation. The success of the program rests in large measure with the trainer's ability to accept without judgment the reactions and comments of parents and to help them see the value of some of the alternatives suggested in this program.

One or more of the exercises that follow may be used as part of the "ice-breaking" process. The trainer must determine which, if any, of these exercises would be useful and workable with his particular group of parents.

ICE BREAKER ACTIVITY — SHARING

Objective

To develop a comfortable climate and readiness for interaction by developing empathy and trust.

Group Size

6-25. When the groups are smaller, there is an increased need for the trainer to maintain an active monitoring role since the experience may become more intense than intended.

Materials

1. Pencils for all
2. Small pad of paper

Time Required

15 minutes for Phase I.
15 minutes for Phase II.

Physical Setting

The group members should be arranged in a circle or around a large conference table. They must not sit in rows for this experience and for the remainder of the program.

TRAINER'S ROLE IN THE PROCESS.   The trainer must be able to provide a comfortable balance between authoritarian and democratic leadership. This means that he must be able to refocus the group's responses to personal feelings to prevent intellectual discussion. Yet, he must stay out of the process as long as the group works at the level of personal feelings. The leader must be prepared to intervene tactfully, sympathetically, and in an accepting manner if one member is taking up more than his share of time.

SETTING THE TONE.   The trainer prepares the group by explaining that in the two sharing experiences that the group will engage in, it will be important to *share feelings* and *experiences* but not opinions and judgments. The purpose of these experiences is not group discussion, in which people give opinions and judgments; rather, it is to share experiences and feelings. The trainer may, depending on the group, lecture briefly on the idea that when a group of people exchange memories, experiences, and feelings, a warmth and closeness usually develops quietly and quickly. This warmth relaxes people so they can better attend to the situation and the things they want to learn because they feel good about the situation.

PHASE I.   All participants are to write down on identical pieces of paper the one thing that concerns or bothers them the most about being in groups such as classes, discussion groups, or groups like the present one. The papers are folded, tossed into a hat, and then mixed up. Each person then takes a turn drawing one of the slips of paper and responding about how he would feel if this were his concern. He should replace his slip if he draws his own. Other participants may join in or add their viewpoints after the initial response. The trainer should monitor pacing so all cards are read within the time allotted. The trainer should encourage such additions by comments such as: "Did anyone have any other feelings or reactions?" or "How do you think you would feel if you had this concern?"

All participants should see that the slips of paper are destroyed at the end of the experience.

PHASE II.   The procedure is the same as in Phase I. However, this time each group member is to write on the slips of paper a brief description of a happy or unhappy event they can remember from their own childhood. The person who draws the slip is to describe how he thinks it would feel to have had that childhood experience: "How would it have affected you?"

The trainer collects and destroys the slips of paper at the end of the experience. This is done without comment.

2

THE FIRST MAJOR KEY:
I AM WORTHWHILE — I AM LOVABLE

INTRODUCTION

The self-concept is one of the most important determinants of behavior. It consists of all the perceptions that a person holds about himself — who he is, what he stands for, what he does, or does not do, and all those things that make him an individual who is unique and separate from all other people. A person with a good self-concept feels that he is worthwhile, capable and important as an individual, while a person with a poor self-concept feels inadequate, incompetent and unimportant. The way a person feels about himself will effect the way he interacts with other people, and will effect the way he performs tasks required of him in his daily living (Quandt, 1973). It is therefore important to look at the various components of self-concept and to teach parents how their behaviors will influence the development of their children's self-concepts.

Self-concept is mostly learned through interacting with other people over long periods of time (Combs and Snyagg, 1959; Purkey, 1970). A child's reactions to experiences are affected more by opinions of significant others than by the mere success or failure of the task itself. The child learns through the approval or disapproval of others whether the task is important to them, whether he is competent at the task, and whether he is a valuable human being (Maehr, 1969). Since parents are the first significant individuals whom a child interacts with, it is important that they be aware that their reactions to their children will influence how those children feel about themselves.

Self-concept has been broken down into two major components for the purpose of discussion in Lessons 2 and 3. These are presented as two major keys, which are basic ways of looking at interactions between a parent and child, in order to determine whether those interactions will increase or decrease a child's positive feelings about himself. The first of these major keys is: "I am Worthwhile — I am Lovable".

From the earliest mother-infant interactions, a child begins to develop a sense of being secure and loved. This feeling of being deeply valued as a person becomes an important precondition for the child to meet the challenges and expectations he encounters later in life (Prescott, 1969). Being loved also makes it possible for the child to learn to love himself and others. If a child has never been loved he cannot fully respect and love himself, and therefore must spend his time reassuring himself as to his fundamental worth as a human being. A deficit in this area is often the foundation for a lifetime of neurotic dysfunctional behavior.

A parent communicates his love for his child in many ways — he provides food, clothing, shelter, he provides for the child's safety, he provides opportunities for learning and growing intellectually, he responds to his child's emotional needs, and he provides discipline and order in his child's life. Every interaction that a parent has with a child is an opportunity for expressing this love and caring, in both verbal and non-verbal ways. A parent's gestures, facial expressions, and general body language can help the child feel loved and cared for, just as much as telling him so.

There are parents who readily say that they truly love their children, and this is not to be doubted, but their children aren't aware of it. Children need to be told how their parents feel about them; they also need praise and encouragement when it is called for, in order for them to learn that they are worthwhile individuals (Adler, 1971). There are also times when children need criticism or discipline, and love and acceptance can be communicated at these times, too.

Haim Ginott (1965) talks about helpful praise and constructive criticism as it is presented in Lesson 2. These are ways of communicating about a child's behavior, without interfering with the child's feelings about himself as a lovable and worthwhile person.

SUMMARY: A child's feelings about himself are learned through the interactions he has with important people in his life, beginning with the very earliest interactions between a mother and her infant. Parent's communicate feelings about their children in many ways — both verbally and non-verbally. The communications are then the basis for the child's learned feelings about himself. It is therefore important that parents be aware of this and learn to communicate in ways to increase their child's positive feelings about himself, which will allow him to face life's demands in a competent manner.

References

1. Adler, M. *A Parent's Manual.* Springfield, Illinois; Chas. C. Thomas, 1971.
2. Combs, A.W. and Snygg, D. *Individual Behavior: A Preceptual Approach to Behavior.* New York: Harper & Row, 1959.
3. Ginott, H. *Between Parent and Child.* New York: The Hearst Corp., 1969. Chapt. 1-3.
4. Maehr, A.C. "Reading and the self-concept." *Elementary English,* 1962, *39*, 210-215, 1962.
5. Quandt, I. *Self-Concept & Reading.* Delaware: International Reading Association, 1974.
6. Prescott, D.A. "Role of Love in Development" in Grebstein, L.C. (Ed.) *Toward Self-Understanding.* Illinois: Scott, Foresman & Co., 1969, pp. 132-136.
7. Purkey, W.W. *Self-Concept and School Achievement.* Englewood Cliffs, NJ: Prentice-Hall, 1970.

Objectives

1. To present the first key idea about how to raise an effective, happy, and loving child. Specifically, whenever possible, the things a parent does with and to his child should help his child come to believe he is worthwhile and lovable.

2. To demonstrate the effects of a parent's verbal and non-verbal behavior upon the child's belief about whether he is a worthwhile and lovable person.

3. To illustrate different methods for praising and criticizing children's behavior. Specifically, "Helpful Praise", and "Constructive Criticism" are presented as two methods which can be used, in communicating with a child so that his self-concept of being a lovable and worthwhile person is not destroyed.

Sequence

1. Lecture-discussion (30-40 minutes)
2. General discussion (20-30 minutes)
3. Discussion of use of workbooks (5-10 minutes)

Special Notes To Trainer

The trainer may encounter difficulty with two exercises in this lesson. Some group members may be reluctant to participate in the Mirror Exercise described in the first half of this lesson. The trainer must be aware that this is a self-confronting experience that comes very early in the program. It is likely that anxiety will be aroused in group members due to the nature of the exercise, and the trainer should be prepared to deal with this. It is important that the trainer urge every group member to participate in the exercise, as it has been found to provide a valuable and insightful experience. This exercise, particularly, has been found to evoke interesting discussions about the disparity between what is communicated in words and what is communicated in gestures and facial expressions.

The verbal explanations of helpful praise and constructive criticism, in the second half of the lesson, may confuse some group members. The blackboard diagram provided in the manual, and any other visual or verbal aids that the trainer wishes to use, are needed to emphasize the two-part, and three-part structures of the two types of communication. It would also be helpful for the trainer to use these techniques in his communications with the parents during the sessions, to serve as a model for them.

The completion of homework assignments from the workbook is very important to the **Parenting Skills** program. The importance of doing their assignments each week must be stressed to the parents, as they serve a major function in each lesson. The success of the first part of each lesson is maximized by the completion of the homework by each parent. The homework also provides additional practice of the skills taught in each lesson, and allows the parent an opportunity to apply their newly-learned skills to their own situations.

The trainer must be sensitive to the motivation and abilities of the members of his group. Writing abilities, reading comprehension levels and attitudes of the participants must be considered when requiring homework assignments. The trainer may need to modify the homework assignments in order to use them with certain groups. This is especially important for groups of parents whose reading and writing skills may hinder them, and inhibit their completion of homework. Depending on the group, the trainer may want to provide some incentive to insure the completion of homework assignments. It cannot be emphasized enough, that the homework is an integral part of the program and must be completed by all parents, if the skills are to be learned.

Materials

1. Blackboard
2. Chalk
3. Eraser
4. 3 mirrors and instructions for mirror exercise

LECTURE·DISCUSSION.   Today we are going to discuss the first of two major ideas in child raising. I believe these ideas are the most important ideas in raising children who will be confident, effective, and loving human beings. The two ideas that I will present during this session and the next I have called the Two Major Keys. These key ideas have come out of the research of psychologists, psychiatrists, and educators and from the wisdom of many successful parents. These keys will be most useful to you as guideposts as you deal with your children. In later sessions we will work on some of the skills you will need to develop in order to put these ideas in action.

The first major key is that your child must develop a beilef that he or she is a **worthwhile** and **lovable** person.

Write these words on board.

These feelings about himself, like every other belief and idea your child will come to have about himself, are **learned.** They form one of the major parts of the self-concept.

Complete the following diagram on the board.

SELF CONCEPT

I am a worthwhile person I am a lovable	Key No. 1
I am a competent person I am a responsible	Key No. 2
All other feelings about self	

When I say his beliefs about himself are learned, I mean that just as a child learns to talk, or read, or play a game, he learns **who he is** by the things people do and say to him.

In a way, a child's parents and the other people around him are like mirrors. When a child does something, the things his parents say to him about it and the expressions on their faces tell him what they think of him. Now, since children are helpless and parents are the source of all the good things such as food, warmth, affection etc., the child cannot reject his parents while he is very young. Therefore, when the parent is angry or annoyed, most children seem to react as though there is something wrong or bad about them. Repeated experiences with an angry, yelling, rough-handling parent slowly teach the child that he is not lovable and worthwhile.

Q. Now, why do you think it is important that the child develop the belief that he is a worthwhile and lovable person?

Pause. Wait for parent responses. Summarize their responses on blackboard.

Yes, all of these are some of the reasons that we must help our children develop this belief. I would like to point out that people who don't believe they are worthwhile or lovable are very often depressed, tired, and lacking in ambition. Depression is the major disorder of our times. Depressed people are people who do not believe they are worthwhile and lovable. Let me give you an example. These are the words of a nineteen-year-old depressed female office worker discussing her feelings about her job and co-workers. Listen carefully to her beliefs about herself as she talks to her therapist.

Patient: "Mary tries to be friendly and helpful, but I just don't have the energy to go shopping during lunchtime."

Therapist: "What do you do?"

Patient: "Well I just hang around the office and try to do a little work. I am not as fast as the other girls. They're really good. (Long pause.) I don't really understand why Mary tries to help. I mean all I do is get in the way and I know I am no fun to be with. I guess she is just a good person and feels pity for me or guilty. (Tears.) God, why do I do these rotten things to people."

The second important reason for helping your child to believe he is lovable and worthwhile is that until your child develops these beliefs, he cannot give love and make others feel worthwhile.

Q. If he can't do these things what do you think his relationships with other people and you will be like?

Pause. Write parental responses on board and summarize their responses using the parents' own words.

Yes, you all seem to have a good appreciation of the importance of this key. I am going to darken the room and I want you to close your eyes and imagine that you are a child again. Think back to when you were between two and six years of age. Imagine that you are in your house and your mother is talking to you. Now, listen carefully while I give you some examples of things that are said to children. I want you to pay attention to how you the child feels. (Pause) Remember, you are the child being spoken to and you need to get in touch with your feelings about what is said.

(Dramatically and sarcastically.):"You just don't care about anybody but yourself. You know I saved that candy for your sister. You're just mean and selfish."

Q. How do you think you would feel about yourself if you were the person being spoken to by this parent whom you loved?

Parent responses. Praise and restate parent responses, pointing out the effects on the person's feelings about himself in terms of his feeling worthwhile and lovable.

(Concerned and interested): "Susie, I know you like to use my pots and I like to share them with you, but please tell me when you want to use them so I won't waste time looking for them."

Q. How do you think you would feel about yourself if you were the person being spoken to by this parent?

Parent responses. Praise and restate parent responses, pointing out the effects on the person's feelings about themselves in terms of being worthwhile and lovable.

These examples were designed to point out the effect our words may be having on our children in terms of the immediate situation and their long-term belief as to whether they are worthwhile or not.

Now I would like for each of you to go to the back of the room where I have set up three mirrors. You are to go three at a time with each of you going to your own mirror. When you get there, there will be a set of directions. Please don't say anything while you are there or when you return. Just read and follow the directions at each mirror. The rest of the class is not to turn around until it is their turn.

Directions at Mirrors

Please be seated. Look into the mirror. Do the following two things. Please try to remember how this exercise feels since we are going to talk about it shortly.

1. Imagine you are talking to your child without saying a word. By using your face, make him or her know you are proud of him and love him. To help you do this exercise, imagine that your child is giving you a present that he just made.

2. This time, using your face, without a word, show him or her that you are annoyed and angry with him or her. To help you do this exercise, imagine yourself walking into your garage and finding your child and his new clothes covered with paint.

Q. Why do you think I asked you to do this exercise?

Restate parent responses. Praise and elaborate as follows:

Yes, all of these things you mentioned are true, but most importantly, I wanted to do this to emphasize and remind you that you communicate to your children not only by what you say but by how you look. Also, the fact that most of you, like most everyone else, found it more difficult to communicate the pride and love than you did the annoyance and anger tells us something. The things we do often feel comfortable and we do with ease, those things which we rarely do often feel strange and uncomfortable. If you found it difficult to communicate pride and love, well now you know something that you can work on to help your child develop his belief that he is a worthwhile, lovable person. You must practice showing love and pride in your face.

Praise and Criticism that Is Not Destructive

We all know that our children will be listening to our words as well as watching our faces when we are communicating with them. It is important to let your child know that you love and respect him, even when he has done something you don't agree with. This must be communicated with words, as well as facial expressions.

Next, we are going to look at the do's" and "don'ts" of talking to your child so that you will help him develop the belief that he is worthwhile and lovable.

When you are talking to your child, it is important to give praise, and at times you will have to give criticism. Both praise and criticism are important, but they should be handled properly.

HELPFUL PRAISE.   To begin, it is important that you learn to praise a person's efforts and ac-complishments accurately without judging the person morally. Statments such as, "You are a good boy," or "You are always honest" often create guilt, and the child cannot accept the praise he deserves because he knows it's not true and it's phony. Praise that is helpful is praise that describes what the child did that was so pleasing.

Write on board: Helpful Praise — describes what the child did and the effects on others.

Helpful Praise

1. What the child did

2. The effects on others

1. _____

2. _____

For example, Johnny helped his mother clean the house before company came without her asking. Using this example I will show you the difference between unhelpful and helpful praise.

(Unhelpful praise):

"Johnny, you are such a good boy. You are always so helpful and thoughtful, I just know I can always depend on you."

(Helpful praise):

I appreciate your helping me dust the furniture. When you help like that, I feel great and it gives me extra time to get ready."

Helpful Praise

1. What the child did
   a. ...helping me dust the furniture

2. The effects on others
   a. ...I feel great, and it gives me extra time to get ready.

This praise is specific; it points out what Johnny did and how it affected others. Let's consider some other examples and decide if the praise is helpful or not.

I appreciate your helping me finish your room by tucking in the blanket on your bed.

Q. Is this helpful praise?

Parent response. (Yes)

2nd example

(Unhelpful praise):

Karen, you always work so hard to help me.

(Helpful praise):

Karen, I appreciate your helping me finish your room by tucking in the blanket on your bed. I really like it when your room is neat.

Helpful praise —

1. Our yard looks nice with all the leaves raked. Thank you for helping me pick up the piles of leaves.
2. I really enjoyed watching your school play. You spoke your lines loud enough for me to hear every word.
3. Jeff, you wrote a very neat homework paper. It was very easy for me to check.

Unhelpful praise —

1. Molly, I'm glad you were a good girl while I was gone.
2. To Jim, who has just brought home a report card with all A's: Oh Jim, you always make me so proud.
3. You did a great job. Thanks for helping.

Next we have a mother on the telephone. She hangs up and says to her four-year-old:

"You are such a good girl. You are always so quiet."

Q. Is this helpful praise?

Parent response. (No)

Q. What would be helpful praise in this situation?

Thank you for being quiet while I was on the telephone, that way I can hear the other person better.

Request examples of helpful praise from parents. Have each parent pick out the two components of helpful praise in their example, and fill in the diagram on helpful criticism.

HELPFUL CRITICISM   Criticism, like praise, is likewise important, but must be handled properly also. Criticism that is not helpful typically attacks the person and doesn't help him see what he did wrong or what he could have done. It also doesn't show the child exactly how what he did affected others.

Write on board: Helpful criticism — describes what a child did wrong, what he could have done, and how it affected others.

Helpful Criticism*

1. Describes what child did   2. The effects on others   3. What he could have done

1. _____   2. _____   3. _____

*Note. For older children age 9 or above it is often best not to include part 3 as stated but rather to ask what else he/she could have done.

Let me give you a few examples:

1. Mark, age five, takes a toy away from his four-year-old brother. Their father steps in and says: "When you will not share any of your toys with your brother, you can't expect him to share any with you."
2. Another father faced with the same situation steps in and says: "Mark, you are being a selfish child. You have no right to steal somebody else's things. If I catch you stealing again you are going to get it but good!"

Q. Which father is using helpful criticism, the first or the second?

Parent response.

Q. Why is the first helpful and the second not?

Parent response

Diagram the first example on the blackboard to demonstrate the three components.

3. Rachel, you were a messy girl today and now we're going to be late for your doctor's appointment.

Q. Is this helpful or unhelpful criticism?

Wait for Response.

Q. What might be some helpful criticism?

"Rachel, I asked you not to go outside after your bath. Now your dress is dirty and we will have to change it before we go to the doctor's. Next time, play inside as I asked you to, because I really don't like to rush to get to the doctor's."

Now let's look at some unhelpful criticism:

"Johnny (age four), you broke the glass because you were a bad boy. You didn't listen to Daddy. Daddy told you three times not to play with it and you broke it on purpose."

Q. What might be some helpful criticism?

Parents response should be accepted and reinforced.

HELPFUL CRITICISM: "Johnny, the glass broke because it was too heavy to carry with one hand. Now you see why Daddy told you to put it down or carry it with two hands. That was in important glass for Daddy and now I am sad that I won't have it any more to use. Well, I guess you had better start cleaning up the mess."

Examples of Unhelpful Criticism

1. I can't stand this fussing anymore. Please go to your rooms and play. I really have a bad headache now.

2. I told you that window would get broken if you played ball so close to the house. What do I have to do to make you listen to me?

3. See what happened because you didn't stop fighting? Your brother is crying and my favorite plant is broken. You should know better than to fight with your brother.

These examples show that parents can praise and criticize their children, but there are helpful ways and destructive ways. The helpful ways don't tear down the child or make him feel that he is a bad person, yet he or she will learn from the criticism.

Later on, during some of the coming sessions, we will work on how to talk to children so that they will talk to you. The ways of talking to children that we will practice will do two things for you. They will help build a close relationship with your child and will help him develop the belief that he is a worthwhile and lovable person.

What I would like you to remember from this session is that the first key to developing a well-adjusted, happy, and loving child is that you must keep in mind as much as possible the following question:

Will what I am doing make my child believe he is a worthwhile and lovable person?

Certainly, you wouldn't have the time to always keep this question in mind. At times you may be angry and will not want to ask yourself such a question, but if you keep this idea in mind most of the time, after a while, it will not be strange. Then it will begin to guide your behavior and you will have made a big step forward in ensuring the future success and happiness of your child.

Q. GENERAL DISCUSSION.   I would like for you to think about what we did during this session.

Q. Does anyone have any questions or reactions?

Pause. Wait for some response. Keep an expectant look on your face and look at the group. Handle all parent's reactions with the following attitude:

Yes, it is difficult. Yes, it is strange. Yes, there are problems with any idea, but if you follow through, I just know it will be helpful to you in the long run.

Help the parent explore how his child may react, and when would be good times to try these new parenting skills.

Q. Would anyone be willing to share an experience with their child in which they think helpful praise or helpful criticism would have been useful?

Pause and allow the parents some time to form a response. Help parents to formulate their responses in the situation, so that they communicate helpful praise, and constructive criticism. Refer to the diagrams on the board. Try to develop as many different responses as possible. By having the parents see that there is not just one right way of giving helpful praise criticism you will increase their comfort in trying to formulate their responses and in using the concept of helpful praise and helpful criticism.

At the end of the general discussion give the parents some directions and information concerning the workbooks and the weekly practice.

DISCUSSION OF USE OF WORKBOOKS.   Before you leave I would like to explain a little about the workbooks and the weekly assignments in them. During our workshops we will discuss some ideas concerning children and our roles as parents. Some of these ideas may be new to you, and some of the skills suggested may be difficult to learn; therefore, we will need time during the week to think about and practice these new ideas and skills. The weekly assignments in your workbook are a must if you are to get full benefit from our sessions. Each week we will start our session by reviewing the home practice assignment for the previous week. During this review it would be most helpful if we shared with each other our experiences and reactions to the assignment.

3

THE SECOND MAJOR KEY:
I AM COMPETENT—I AM RESPONSIBLE

Introduction

The second basic component of a child's self-concept is a feeling of being competent and responsible. We have seen that children learn that they are lovable and worthwhile human beings through the communications from their parents and other significant people. They also learn a self-concept as to whether they are competent and responsible human beings. Just as feelings of self-worth influence a child's behavior, so do his beliefs about his competence and his sense of responsibility.

Competence is an attitude about one's self that is developed through repeated interactions with people and the environment. It is a feeling and an expectation of having sufficient skill, knowledge, or experience to cope with a situation in an appropriate and adequate manner. At the moment of birth an infant possesses certain capabilities or competencies — he is capable of developing language, he is capable of producing behavior in others related to his own actions, he is capable of acting on his environment to get a response. For example, crying and smiling, are efficient tools for building attachments with his caretakers, and for getting help for his needs (Gordon, 1975). Throughout the rest of his early development, a child gains competency in motor skills, mental skills, language skills, and interpersonal and social skills, as a result of his transactions and communications with both his physical and personal-social worlds.

The skills that a child masters and the feeling of competence that he develops as a result of positive feedback from others and himself about the worth of these skills and his mastery of them, are important factors in a child's future accomplishments. His approach to new experiences, and the acquisition of new skills will be influenced by the child's actual competence and his *sense* of competence (Gordon, 1975). With a positive sense of competence as a base, a child will more likely be willing to try new tasks (White, 1959).

Most people will agree that adequate preparation for life requires a sense of responsibility (Dinkmeyer and McKay, 1973). This follows hand-in-hand with a sense of competence. As a child tries new experiences and ventures into new areas of learning, he soon finds out that he is capable of causing things to happen — both good and bad. In other words, he is repsonsible for certain events; if he has a sense of competence he will feel that he is in control of the results of his behavior, and thus is "responsible".

It is commonly felt that parents must *teach* responsibility to their children through the use of punishment and rewards, for various behaviors (Dinkmeyer and McKay, 1973). Responsibility cannot be taught, however; it must be given to the child in such a way that it allows him to learn how to handle it, without jepardizing his sense of self-worth and competence. The child must be provided with opportunities to experience and learn the natural consequences of his behavior. These opportunities must be provided without the threat of harsh punishment.

The parent who performs tasks for this child because he can do it more quickly, or simply better, or because he does not like for his child to suffer failures and frustrations, is taking away the child's opportunities to learn competence and responsibility. It is obvious that a balance must be struck between abandoning the child to cope with tasks and situations beyond his ability and allowing the child to struggle and cope with some problems.

SUMMARY: Competency and responsibility make up the second major component of the self-concept. A child learns that he is competent through a mastery of various developmental tasks, and through the response of others to his ability to master these tasks. Responsibility is learned by the child as he is allowed to experience and to become aware of the consequences of his actions. If this occurs in an atmosphere of love and acceptance, as well as a respect for the competence of the child, he will learn that he is responsible for performing certain tasks for himself and others. He will also learn to perform socially-expected behaviors, and will do these willingly without parental pressure.

References

1. Dinkmeyer, D. and Mckay, G.D. *Raising a Responsible Child.* New York: Simon and Schuster, 1973.

2. Dreikurs, R. and Grey, L. *A Parents Guide to Child Discipline.* New York: Hawthorne Books, 1970.

3. Gordon, I.J. *The Infant Experience.* Columbus, Ohio: Charles E. Merrill Publishing Company, 1975.

4. White, R.W. *"Motivation Reconsidered: The Concept of Competence."* Psychology Review, 1959, 66, 297-333.

Objectives

1. To show parents the importance of the child's development of competence and to develop the parent's understanding that their interactions with their child will influence this development.

2. To teach parents how they can help their children to feel competent and in control of the results of their behavior.

3. To teach parents that they can guide their children in accepting responsibility by allowing them to recognize the consequences of their actions.

SPECIAL NOTES TO TRAINEES. Time must be allowed by the trainer for a review and sharing of homework from Session 2. Each member should be encouraged to offer their responses to the homework activities, and to raise any questions they had. The trainer should encourage and reinforce the discussion, so that members will feel that this part of the session is just as important as the learning of new material. Their understanding of the information presented in Session 2 is critical to their learning the concepts presented in Session 3.

The second half of this lesson is the most difficult to teach. This section is devoted to demonstrating 4 different ways a parent can behave in order to foster the development of a sense of competence and responsibility in their child:

1. Non-interacting or interfering, but being present and accepting the child's efforts.

2. Using helpful praise and constructive criticism.

3. Altering the situation to assist the child to cope with it.

4. Helping the child experience the logical consequences of his behavior.

The first method, non-interacting, non-interfering is often initially objected to. Most parents see themselves as teachers of their children and the idea of allowing a child to make a mistake, or do something which isn't the best way, frequently upsets them. The trainer needs to be sensitive to objections from group members and be prepared to deal with them. One method that seems to be effective, is to have the parent get in touch with what the child's feelings are in a particular situation. Specifically the parent is to think what he would be saying to himself while his parent was correcting him or showing him a better way. The importance of the idea is that while a parent thinks he is helping, he may actually be giving the child the message that he failed again, or that he can't do anything right, and is incompetent. The issue is not whether parental correction or instruction is needed or helpful, it certainly is, but rather the kind and frequency of parental feedback and correction.

Materials

1. Blackboard
2. Chalk
3. Eraser

Sequence

1. Review and sharing of home practice (20-30 minutes)
2. Lecture-discussion (20-30 minutes)
3. General discussion (20-30 minutes)

REVIEW AND SHARING OF HOME PRACTICE   Last week we discussed the First Major Key: I am worthwhile — I am lovable. We learned some ways of communicating love and acceptance as well as criticism. These ways of communicating, as you remember, were called "helpful praise" and "helpful criticism."

Put the diagram used in Lesson 2 on the blackboard. Review with the parents the two components of helpful praise and the three components of helpful criticism.

Q. Ask if anyone would be willing to share their home practice with the group.

Pause. Wait for a volunteer. If none comes forth within 10-15 seconds, urge the parents to respond by explaining that the sharing of our ideas and experiences is one of the best ways of helping both ourselves and each other since hearing how another person does things helps us get new ideas. If resistance remains, you should deal with the parents' feelings about sharing, embarrassment, appearing foolish, etc.

Use the diagram on the board to discuss the examples provided by the parents.

LECTURE-DISCUSSION   Today we are going to talk about the second key idea for helping you to raise your child to be happy and successful in life. The idea we are going to talk about is **competence.** Now this key idea means that your child must come to believe that he is competent. Psychological research has shown that if a person believes he is competent, he will be more satisfied with himself, more persistent in solving problems, more willing to try new things, more willing to learn, more able to see that he can change his world (or at least part of it), and more resistant to depression and anxiety. He will achieve higher grades in school and be more likely to accept responsibility for what he does.

Write on blackboard: Competence.

Q. Now, what does competence mean to you? When and where does it show itself?

Abbreviate responses and write answers on blackboard. The following idea must be pointed out:

We develop our sense of competence from everything we do — social conversation, reading and other school work, playing games, getting around, helping ourselves, arts and crafts, etc.

Now, fortunately or unfortunately, children learn and develop not only a sense of competence about themselves as game players, good talkers, good readers, etc., but they also collect all their feelings of competence or incompetence, and they develop some overall idea of whether they are competent or incompetent.

Q. How do you think a child who feels competent will behave in the following situation?

1. Meeting a new neighbor.

Give time for class response.

Yes, he probably would go up and introduce himself and make friends.

2. Becoming involved in a class play.

    Class response.

Yes, he probably would work hard to get a part in the play and the most important part possible.

3. Being sent to the store to buy something.

    Class response.

Yes, he would see the trip to the store as a way to prove himself. He would be delighted in parent's recognition of his maturity.

4. Being left with a babysitter.

    Class response.

He would see this as a person he could have fun with, learn things from, do things with, get to do things for him.

Q. Now, how do you think a child who feels incompetent will behave in these same situations?

1. Meeting a new neighbor.

    Class response. Summarize and reflect responses of group.

2. Becoming involved in a class play.

    Class response. Summarize and reflect responses of group.

3. Being sent to the store to buy something.

    Class response. Summarize and reflect responses of group.

4. Being left with a babysitter

    Class response. Summarize and reflect responses of group.

Okay, now we have examined the idea that competence is the second major key to raising a happy and successful child. You can all see that whether a child believes that he is competent or not will affect how he behaves and what he does. Which child would you prefer—a competent one or an incompetent one?

    Pause.

Well, how you handle your child in a thousand little situations will determine the difference.

You will not always be able to handle situations such that they will help your child develop a broad feeling of competence. However, if you keep the competence key in mind at least 51 percent of the time, you will make a real difference in your child's life. You must ask yourself: What will the effect of what I am doing be on my child's sense of competence? Will it make him or her believe he or she is competent or incompetent?

Now we have the basic ideas, but let's see if we can examine it more closely so that we can see how you could put this idea to work for your child in everyday situations.

Two ways you can assist your child in developing his sense of competence are: first to reinforce or encourage his efforts to do things; second by making his world—your home—easier to deal with. Now, let's consider each of these ideas one at a time.

Reinforcing or encouraging your child's efforts to do things means that you appreciate what your child accomplishes and you do not focus on the parts of his behavior that are not successful. For example, when a child begins to use a spoon, his mother would reinforce his efforts with comments such as "What a big boy you are feeding yourself." This reinforcement, encouragement, is given despite the fact that the spoon is held wrong, and he gets half of the food on his cheeks and chin. But this child's mother could say: "No, Jimmy, you are holding the spoon wrong. Look, do it like Mommy. Careful, you are making a mess." What Jimmy's mother has said in this example tells him many things — including the idea that his behavior is not acceptable and he isn't doing well. Let's consider some other examples.

Sally's father was watching her painting a picture. He noticed that she was about to use purple paint to color a little boy's hair, and he said:

"No, Sally. Who ever heard of someone with purple hair? Use black or brown to color his hair."

Q. What was Sally's father telling her?

Pause. Wait for class response.

Yes, Sally's father was saying that he didn't like the way she was painting her picture, and that she wasn't doing it right. Listen to another example.

John's mother sent him to the store to buy a loaf of bread. When he came back empty-handed she said: "John, why can't you ever do as I ask. I will just have to do everything myself. What an inconvenience!" What did John's mother say to him about his competence?

Pause. Wait for response.

Yes, John's mother was saying that he was not competent, and she would have to do everything herself, so that it would be done right.

Three-year-old Robin is having a birthday party. Her mother is in the living room with the party guests when she sees Robin coming around the corner with a plate full of cookies and one of them drops to the floor. Robin's mother jumps up and rushes over to take the plate out of Robin's hand. She says: "Here, dear, let me take that. You might spill them. Go on over and play with your friends. I'll pass the cookies around."

Q. What do you think the mother in this example was teaching her daughter about her competence?

Pause. Class response.

Yes, from Robin's point of view her mother was saying you can't handle the situation, Robin. I can't trust you, you're not competent.

Q. How might Robin's mother respond in order to help Robin develop a sense of competence?

Pause. Class response.

EXAMPLE OF CONSTRUCTIVE RESPONSES   1) She might have just stayed where she was and given Robin a broad smile of approval and pride. Or, 2) she might have said: "Thank you for your help, Robin. It's nice to have someone who can help me."

Now, if Robin's mother would have responded in one of the last two ways, what would the risk have been? Yes, the cookies could have been spilled, but this seems a minor consequence and risk for the possible step forward in the development of Robin's sense of competence and personal pride. I often have found that when situations such as the one described are cast in the light of a child's personal development as opposed to a model of efficiency to get a job done, all parents will choose to do what will help their child develop a sense of competence. No mother would choose a dozen cookies over giving her child a memory of competence and acceptance.

Let me describe a situation and then let's see if you can provide a reaction that will reinforce and encourage the child in such a way as to build his sense of competence.

Billy, age six, is working in the basement of his house. His father is awakened by the pounding of a hammer and comes down to see what's happening. He opens the door and sees nails all over the floor and Billy working on building a lopsided box with all four sides of different lengths, not fitting together and with bent nails sticking out of the wood.

Q. What might Billy's father say if he wanted to help Billy's sense of competence?

Pause. Class response. If parents don't come up with some constructive examples, give some.

EXAMPLES OF THINGS HE COULD DO   Well, he might just stand there and smile, with an interested look on his face and say nothing, or he might say: "What are you making, Billy?" Billy could tell him and then he would say: "It sure looks hard to make. Let me know when it's done." Then father walks away.

Q. What are the risks here?

Pause. Class response.

Yes, Billy could possibly cut his hand or hit his finger with the hammer. But maybe it is worth it to have the pride and sense of competence that comes from doing it yourself.

Some people will think that the ideas expressed don't make sense because children need some instructions. I agree that some instruction is needed, and possibly Billy's father could have given him one suggestion. However, all to often parents overinstruct the child by telling him too much for that day. I would suggest that as a rule of thumb when you want to instruct your child who is working on a project, volunteer no more than one suggestion per hour. Your suggestions would be best expressed as follows: "Billy, do you think putting the box in the vise would make it easier to work on?"

Pause.

Q. Do you have any questions or reactions to what I have just said?

Wait for parents reactions and discuss their concerns.

Now let's move on to consider how you can manage your child's world (your home) and his behavior in it to assist in his developing a sense of competence.

If we consider your home or your young child's world there are certain things that you can do to this world to help his sense of competence. First, you can try to fix things so that the child can meet his needs and responsibilities considering his size, strength, and muscle coordination. The following are examples of some changes in the child's world that parents have made to ecourage their child's sense of competence and independence:

1. Putting a bench in the bathroom so that the child can get his own glass of water.
2. Putting big tags on zippers so that the child can open and close his own zippers.
3. Making a top sheet and blanket for his bed with corners on the foot end like a form-fitted sheet so that the child can more easily make his own bed.
4. Placing a large box in his room for toys instead of using drawers and shelves.

Q. What are some things **you** might do to make it easier for your child to act competently and independently?

Wait for parents' responses.

Before considering the idea of responsiblity through consequences I would like to summarize what has been said so far: It is important for the parent to help the child feel that he is capable of handling situations that he comes into contact with. After having experienced feelings of competance in his activities, he will begin to face new situations with the belief that he will be able to master them. With time, he will come to see himself as competent and this will support his positive feelings about himself.

This brings us to the idea that the child must learn to be responsible — to be willing to accept responsibility for his actions. As parents, we can assist the child in recognizing that he is competent and that he does have consequences. The consequences of his actions, whether they be positive or negative, acceptable or unacceptable, are the fruits of his labor. The child must learn to accept responsibility through the consequences of his behavior. If he doesn't like the consequences, he will learn to do someting different next time. Let's consider some examples of consequences that are likely to teach responsibility.

Three-year-old Timmy was playing outside and stepped into a mud puddle. His shoes got all wet, so he comes into the house, dripping wet, for some dry clothes. When he asked if he could go outside again, his shoes were still wet, so his mother said very calmly in a matter of fact manner:

"I'm sorry, Timmy, you cannot go outside because your shoes are still wet."

Notice that Timmy's mother pointed out the consequence of his behavior and, thus, his responsibility. She didn't say: "No, you were a bad boy and got your shoes wet." Rather, she said: "I'm sorry, Timmy, you cannot go outside because your shoes are still wet." She did not have to give him a lecture on how he would be likely to catch a cold or how he should have been more careful and should not have gotten himself all wet. What is really important is that now Timmy will see that what he did — getting his shoes and himself all wet — leads to his not being able to go outside. Because he probably doesn't like the consequence, he is more likely to learn not to get his shoes wet.

This idea seems like a very simple thing to do, but you will find that it's hard to put into practice. Parents are used to punishing "bad behavior" — getting angry, yelling, and scolding. Simply letting Timmy see that he can't play outside because of his own actions, helps the parent avoid getting upset. Without the emotional upset of his parent to respond to, Timmy will be better able to see that he alone is the one responsible for his actions.

If a parent is going to be able to help his child learn to accept responsibility for his behavior, the parent will need to react to situations that occur by pointing out the consequences of the child's behavior in a way that is not nasty. Unfortunately, all too often people respond to irresponsible behavior with an aggressive manner like: "Now, I've got you." In building the child's sense of responsibility, it is importnat that both positive as well as negative consequences be pointed out, and it is best to point out more positive consequences than negative consequences.

An example of pointing out positive consequences of the child's behavior is a mother admiring a picture in a coloring book the child has just finished. She might say something like: "You worked slowly and carefully on this picture and it looks very neat and pretty." We see that the mother has pointed out to the child the results of his behavior — it looks neat and pretty.

Pause

A child came home from school with a big smile and excitedly told her mother that she had the highest score on a spelling assignment. "Look, Mommy, the teacher even wrote 'Excellent' on my paper."

"That's great," said the mother. "You worked very hard for that test last night and you made an excellent mark. You should be very proud of yourself."

The mother has pointed out to the girl the consequence of her behavior: She worked very hard, thus getting a high mark, and deserves to feel pride in her work, not in making Mommy proud.

Now let's consider an instance of a parent pointing out a negative consequence. Danny and his father decided to go out to play ball. "Where is the ball, Danny?" asked the father. Danny shrugged his shoulders and said he couldn't find it.

To this his father said: "You didn't put your ball back in the toy box and now we

*can't find it and we can't play ball." The father has pointed out the boy's actions
and the consequences of that behavior.*

Q. What was the behavior that led to the consequence pointed out by the father?

Pause. Class response. (Not putting the ball back in the toy box.)

Q. And what was the consequence of not putting the ball away?

Pause. Class response. (Not being able to find it and not being able to play.)

Right. By showing Danny that his behavior of not putting the ball away led to the
consequence of not being able to find it and thus not being able to play, the father is
demonstrating to Danny that he is responsible for his behavior and the consequences of
that behavior.

We can never escape all of the conflicts that we may have with our children. But we can
help them to see that they are responsible for their actions since their behavior brings
about certain results. We must as parents help guide our children in their learning of
responsibility by keeping calm and letting them experience the results of their behavior.

GENERAL DISCUSSION

Q. Are there any questions or reactions? Can anyone see how they might use some of
these ideas?

During the coming week I would like you to consider the ideas presented in this week's
session. You all have a home practice assignment that you should work on at different
times during the week. Don't plan to sit down and do all the home practice at one sitting.
Please bring your workbooks to class next week and to all future sessions. We will start
our session next week by reviewing the home practice assignments.

4

EVALUATING THE PARENT-CHILD RELATIONSHIP

Objectives

1. To help parents realize that their effectiveness in guiding their child's behavior depends on the quality of the parent-child relationship.
2. To help parents understand the concepts of **effectiveness** and **power** as they relate to child management techniques and to be able to analyze their own child management methods in terms of these two concepts.
3. To help parents assess the quality of the relationship they have with their child.

SPECIAL NOTES TO TRAINERS   The first section of Lesson 4 introduces the ideas of effectiveness and power in child management. This may be a difficult distinction to make for some parents who hold the belief that a parent needs to be forceful and firm in order to make children behave. This may lead into a discussion of the virtues of a forceful vs. a permissive approach to handling children. However, the trainer should steer away from such a debate, and emphasize to the group that "effectiveness" is more important than the logical merits of any one strategy. A discussion focusing on effectiveness allows the parents to see that there is not a right and a wrong way to interact with children in every circumstance, but rather a number of effective and ineffective ways of interacting.

Related to the notion of effectiveness, is the idea that the effectiveness of any technique will be dependent upon the quality of the parent-child relationship. The analogy of a savings account which is used to discuss the differences between a positive and negative relationship has proven to be a helpful technique.

The second portion of Lesson 4 is designed to help the parents recognize cues that might indicate that their relationship with their child is positive or negative. The trainer should encourage parents to suggest their own cues, and not rely solely on the examples provided. However, parents may be reluctant to respond because they might be embarrassed, or appear incompetent, especially when discussing cues for a negative relationship. It will be very helpful for the trainer to share openly some of his own experiences, particularly negative ones, in order to help the parents feel more comfortable in examining their relationship with their child.

One particular cue for a positive parent-child relationship, is the open expression of feelings between parent and child. If the feelings being expressed are pleasant or positive, parents know that this is a sign of a good relationship. However, they have difficulty understanding how the expression of hostile, angry or other negative feelings can be a positive sign. The trainer, therefore, must emphasize that open communication of feelings, and the attitude of freedom to express oneself, regardless of context is the positive aspect of this communication. It should be explained that, even though a parent may not always agree, or approve of what their child says, it is important to let the child know he is loved and accepted enough to express his feelings. Later lessons will show parents ways to deal with negative communications.

Materials

1. Large Blackboard
2. Chalk

3. Eraser
3. Pencils for all parents

Reference (for Trainers)

Trieschman, A.E., Whittaker, J.K., and Brendtro, L.K., *The Other 23 Hours.* Chicago: Aldine Publishing Co., 1969, Chapter 2.

Sequence

1. Review and sharing of home practice (20-30 minutes)
2. Lecture-discussion (40-50 minutes
   a. Lecture on effectiveness and force and the parent-child relationship.
   b. Group discussion of signs of a positive relationship
   c. Lecture on signs of a negative relationship
   d. Group discussion of examples supplied by leader
3. General discussion (10-15 minutes)

REVIEW AND SHARING OF HOME PRACTICE

Q. Would someone be willing to share their reactions to the home practice assignment? All members of the group should get a chance to speak and share their homework experiences.

LECTURE-DISCUSSION   During most of our remaining sessions we will be talking about skills parents can use in managing children. Parents often worry about the techniques they use to guide and discipline their children. They worry because they know how important their job as a parent is, and they know they can be very good at it or very bad at it. Parents can often recognize that a certain approach is helpful or not, but it is more difficult and also more important to know *why* what they did was helpful or not. Let's look at two examples of ways to handle a problem in managing children.

Billy, who is six, and his younger brother Jimmy are playing in their bedroom. Mom and Dad are trying to watch the news on TV but are annoyed by the boys' loud playing. The noise from the boys' room gets louder and louder. Finally, Dad rushes into the room and tells the boys to quit being noisy or he will spank them and send them to bed. He leaves the room to return to the TV show. At first the boys are quiet, but in a few minutes the noise is as loud and distracting as before.

Let's look at another approach to handling the same problem. Once again the boys are being very loud. This time when Dad walks in the room, he says: "What are you playing, boys?"

"Jimmy is a ghost and he's trying to catch me."

"Sounds like fun, but you know your mother and I are watching the news and I can't hear because it's so noisy in here."

"We'll try to be quieter."

Dad returns to his show and the boys are quieter.

Everybody can tell which is the good example and which is the bad example, but remember the important thing is why. What is different in the two approaches? One difference is that in the first example, the father was not successful in getting the boys to be quieter. Threatening to spank the boys and send them to bed made them quieter for a couple of minutes, but they were soon as noisy as they had been before. We can say that this approach was not effective. The second approach was effective. The father wanted the boys to be quieter and after he talked to them, they were quieter. So one way these two approaches differed was in how effective they were. A second way they differed was in the amount of force used. Threatening physical punishment is an approach that contains a great deal of force. Explaining how the boys' behavior is interfering with your watching a TV show is an approach that contains very little force. Everytime one person wants another one to do something, a certain amount of force is used. The amount of force can be very high or it can be very low. When a robber stops you and threatens to shoot you if you don't hand over your money, he is using a great deal of force. When your wife or husband says they would rather not go to the movie tonight, but they will go if you really want to, they are using very little force. Let's look at the effectiveness and the amount of force in another situation.

Mom and Dad are relaxing in the living room and their daughter, Becky, is in her room listening to her record player. She turns the volume very high and it begins to annoy her parents. Mother goes to Becky's room and says: "Becky, I can't relax when your record is so loud. It hurts my ears and I can feel myself getting angry." Becky says "okay" but in a few minutes, the record player is as loud as before. This time Dad walks in the room, pulls the plug out, and puts the record player on the shelf where Becky can't reach it. He says: "Now maybe you'll learn we mean it when we ask you to something!" Becky begins to cry and sob and shout "I hate you" at her parents. This lasts about five minutes, and of course, no one feels relaxed.

Q. Can someone tell us how these two approaches differ in force and effectiveness?

Pause. Wait for response.

Yes, mother's approach was low force and low effectiveness, while father's approach was high force and low effectiveness.

In this situation we have two approaches to the same problem. Force and effectiveness are two very important issues in deciding what are good and bad ways to manage children. The issue of effectiveness is easy to understand. Parents always want to be effective in guiding their children. The issue of force is a little less clear. To understand why force is an important issue in selecting ways to manage children, we will have to talk about parent-child relationships. The feelings of good will, appreciation, respect, and love, which are shared by parents and children, can be looked at as being like money in a savings account. As conflicts arise, positive feelings are withdrawn from the account. Sometimes, it seems that children have fired their parents and no longer look to their parents as sources of guidance and support. When this happens, the good feelings are withdrawn little by little until there is no money left in the account, and the parent-child relationship is bankrupt. There are no positive feelings left to help resolve the conflicts.

If needed, diagram this analogy on the board.

Deposits	Withdrawals	Empty Account	Full Account
	punishment		love
helpful	unhelpful	negative	respect
praise	criticism	parent-child	
		relationship	
attention	rejection		
	not listening to		

Let's look at some of the consequences of good and bad parent-child relationships.

Sally and her mother get along wonderfully together. They enjoy each other's company and respect each other's feelings. One day Sally's mother was planning to have some of her girl friends over to play bridge and chat. She was running a little behind schedule and she said to Sally: "I'm afraid I'm not going to be ready when my friends arrive." Sally said: "I'll do the dishes, will that help?"

Mrs. Jones and her daughter Karen don't seem to get along very well together. One afternoon Mrs. Jones said: "Karen, would you help me with these dishes so I can get the house cleaned up before my friends come over." Karen answered: "I'll be right there." Ten minutes later, Karen still had not come to help with the dishes.

Sally's mother and Karen's mother both tried to get their daughters to help them. They both tried to use low-force techniques, but low-force methods only work when there is love and respect in the account. Sally's mother could draw on the affection and mutual respect in her relationship with her child. But when the account is bankrupt, as it was for Mrs. Jones and Karen, then it is impossible to draw from it.

Use these examples within the context of the bank diagram to explain the analogy if needed.

There is another very important point to be seen in these examples. Both mothers used the same technique, but one was effective and one was not. The reason for this difference was the difference in the quality of the parent-child relationship. And this is the important point. How effective any technique will be in managing and guiding a child's behavior depends on the quality of the relationship between parent and child. How effective you will be in managing and guiding your child's behavior depends on how much affection and respect is invested in your parent-child relationship. And this is why force is an important issue in how you manage your children. Using force is like drawing money out of your account. The greater the amount of force used, the greater is the cost to your relationship. In fact, the amount of force used by parent and by child is one indication of how good the parent-child relationship is.

Remember the issue is primarily the effectiveness of the parents' actions. There are times in which force or power are needed and the parent will find himself disciplining his child.

Q. Are there any reactions, comments or questions about what has been said so far?

Entertain questions.

When all questions have been answered, begin a discussion of how children show their parents that they love and respect them.

Leader initiates group discussion by saying:

"What are some of the ways your children signal to you that they like you or respect you or are happy that you are their parents?"

If response is not forthcoming within about 30 seconds, supply an example such as:

"My little girl shows me her coloring work and then tells me 'It's for you.' She thinks I am someone she can share her accomplishments with."

Get as many examples as you can. The list may include: child demonstrates affection either verbally or nonverbally, child shows concern for the parent's feelings either verbally or by his behavior, child's play expresses themes of parent-child warmth, child seeks parent's assistance in difficult tasks, child shares accomplishments with parent, child models parent behavior.

You may also have an opportunity to emphasize that different parental values will influence the perception of the child's behavior as positive or negative. Then make a list on the board of answers obtained from parents. Supply examples for categories that may not come up.

As you can see there are really quite a variety of ways young children can let you know that they care about you. Of course, each child develops his own methods of telling you that he values his relationship with you. If you can tune into your child's expressions of affection and respect, then you have one way of knowing that you have a positive relationship.

Pause.

Q. Would anyone be willing to share some expressions of affection used by their children?

Pause.

There are also ways to tell if your relationship is bankrupt.

I'd like to describe for you some of the things to look for that can indicate that your relationship with your child is in danger of being bankrupt. Then we will look at some examples of parent-child interactions and see what you know about assessing the quality of a parent-child relationship. I'll mention five signs of trouble in the parent-child relationship.

The first is the absence of the good signs that we discussed earlier, no messages of affection and caring.

Write on board: 1. No messages of affection.

Of course it could mean that you have not tuned into the messages your child is sending.

The second indication of trouble is if your self-talks, the sentences you tell yourself about situations, are not sensible, then you may find that your child is often in trouble in your eyes. For example, if you say to yourself, "People should always put the cap back on the toothpaste tube," and allow yourself to get angry when someone forgets, then it is likely that you will often be angry at your child since children often forget. If you frequently experience negative emotions concerning your child's behavior, then your relationship may be in trouble.

Write on board: 2. Nonsense self-talks.

The third sign of trouble is when minor problems become catastrophes. This is an indication of a relationship that is failing. For example when a lost pair of mittens can set off a parent-child squabble that lasts for days, and when three weeks later, the whole incident is brought up again, then the parent-child relationship is in trouble.

Of course, this can work both ways. For example a child can turn a small disappointment into evidence that the whole world is against him.

Write on board: 3. Small problem becomes catastrophe.

A fourth sign of relationship problems involves the way you talk to your child. Certain types of communication can be destructive to a parent-child relationship. For example, little Stuart is pretending that he is baking a cake and his father says: "What are you, some kind of sissy?" Father's name-calling lets Stuart know he is not accepted. This loosens the bonds of affection. Name-calling is one example of destructive communication. Others are saracasm, lecturing, threatening, shaming, and blaming.

Destructive communications are those communications which attack the child's sense of being worthwhile or competent.

Write on board: 4. Destructive communications.

The fifth sign of parent-child relationship problems is the frequent use of high-force methods in dealing with children.

Write on board: 5. Frequent use of high force.

As was mentioned earlier, when there is love and respect in the relationship account, then these good feelings can be drawn on to influence how your child behaves. If your child cares for you and cares about your feelings, then you have a very powerful, very effective, low-force method of managing his behavior. If he wants to maintain his good relationship with you, he can be influenced by simply knowing how you feel about what he is doing. Within limits, he will continue to do things that he knows please you and he will avoid doing things that he knows do not please you. When the relationship is strong, many issues can be handled by low-force methods.

Q. Does anyone have any reaction to these five signs that they would be willing to share with the class?

Pause for reactions.

Okay, I've written out some examples of situations that contain a signal about a parent-child relationship.

Pass out handout.

I'll read the situation and I'd like you to tell me how good the parent-child relationship is in each situation and what makes you think so. You must assume that the pattern of behavior characterizes the parent-child relationship.

Read first situation, etc.

1. Beth is playing with her dolls. The mother doll says to the baby doll: "Would you like to go th the park, honey?" "Oh, yes," says the baby doll.

   Guide group discussion. (Answer: positive — child is expressing positive feeling in play theme.)

2. "If I hear that one more time, I'm sending you to bed without any supper."

   (Answer: negative — excessive force.)

3. Mary says: "When I get big, I want to be a mother. That would be really neat."

   (Answer: positive — sees being a mother as a positive role.)

4. Peter forgot to put his bike on the porch. Father says: "I guess you don't know how to take care of your bike. I'm going to put it in the garage and I don't want you to ride it for two weeks."

   (Answer: negative — excessive force, severe punishment for minor transgression.)

5. Billy, age 5, has just told his mother he hates her. Mother spanks him, saying: "You don't talk to me like that, you brat. You ever smart-mouth me again and you won't sit down for a week."

   (Answer: negative — punishing child for expressing important feeling, teaching child not to share feelings.)

6. Sara says to her father: "Is it all right if I tell you something?" Father says: "Sure it is." Sara says: "I don't like Benjamin."

   (Answer: positive and negative sign — child does share her feelings with her father, but she is not quite sure she can.)

7. Mother says to 10-year-old Scott: "Please take your thumb out of your mouth. Only babies suck their thumbs."

   (Answer: negative sign — mother is shaming child, attacking his sense of being worthwhile.)

8. It has been a bad day for Tony. He forgot to take his lunch to school and then he got into a fight with another boy and the teacher made him stay inside during recess. When he gets home from school, he goes straight to his room and stays there until his mother tells him it is time for supper.

   (Answer: negative — child cannot share bad feelings with mother and mother expresses no interest in his "sad" behavior.

9. Amy says to her father: "Daddy, can ghosts fly through walls at night?"

   (Answer: positive — child is sharing her feelings of fear at least tentatively.)

10. Shelly comes home from school and says to her mother: "I hate that fat old teacher. I wish I didn't have to go to school.

    (Answer: positive sign — the child can share unpleasant feelings with mother.)

GENERAL DISCUSSION   Can anyone think of a sign or signal that tells them when things are going well or poorly in their relationship with their children? Would anyone be willing to share that sign or signal with us?

Now during the next week I want all of you to tune into the signals between yourself and your child which tell you something about how strong your relationship is. When you notice something that seems to give some indication about the relationship, write it down on the paper I will give you and bring these examples to class next week.

5

BUILDING YOUR RELATIONSHIP WITH YOUR CHILD:
PART I — COMMUNICATING LOVE AND ACCEPTANCE

Objectives

1. To convey the importance of the quality of the parent-child relationship in terms of love and acceptance.
2. To teach the parent four ways of communicating love and acceptance.

SPECIAL NOTES TO TRAINER   The important point of this lesson is that it is not enough for a parent to love and accept his child. He must demonstrate his love and acceptance, in all interactions, whether the child is being praised or scolded. The trainer should emphasize that this requires active steps on the part of the parent, rather than a passive assumption that a child knows he is loved because all parents love their children.

Of the four methods described as ways to communicate love and acceptance, the idea of joining into a child's activity when invited, and doing so as a workman, seems to be the most difficult for parents to understand. The trainer should explore with the parents their feelings about reversing roles with their child. The trainer needs to allow time for discussion about this issue. Some parents seem to feel threatened at the idea of giving their child the opportunity to be in control; and of being placed in a one-down position. This point specifically may be brought out in a general way to the group as a way of opening up the discussion. The trainer can also be helpful as a model to the group, by placing himself in one-down situations with various group members as the opportunities arise. Acknowledging a parent's expertise and knowledge, allowing a parent to explain or re-explain a concept to the group, etc. are ways of allowing the parents to take control within the group in order to model this concept. While it is important to recognize that there may be some activities which are harmful to the child's well-being in which parents must intervene, there are numberous opportunities for parents to allow their child to continue with their activity undisturbed and in a leadership role in relation to the parent.

Materials

1. Blackboard
2. Chalk
3. Eraser
4. 3 x 5 cards and pencils for each parent

Sequence

1. Review and sharing of home practice (20-30 minutes)
2. Lecture-discussion (20-30 minutes)
3. General discussion (20-30 minutes)

REVIEW AND SHARING OF HOME PRACTICE

Q. Would someone be willing to share the results of their home practice assignment with us?

Q. Did you have any specific problems or reactions to the assignment?

Encourage all the parents to share their home practice, but be careful not to pressure them. This must be a voluntary act.

LECTURE-DISCUSSION   How do our children know that we love them? That we like them? That we accept them? These are the questions I want to focus on in this session, and I believe there is a wide variety of ways that we can answer them.

It seems to me that parents are expected to love their children. Yet when I read any newspaper, I sometimes wonder about the relationships in some homes. What I mean is: kids are running away, kids are getting in trouble, kids are harming their families, and on and on. Now I don't believe that the parents of these children didn't love them. In fact, I have not yet met a set of parents who didn't love and care about their children. What I wonder about is if the kids knew that mom and dad loved them and accepted them.

Now if I asked you right this moment how you could let your children know that you loved them, I'm sure you'd give me an obvious answer. The straightforward answer would probably be that you'd tell them — I love you, son, or I love you, daughter.

It will probably be no big news story to you when I say that telling is not enough. Merely saying "I love you" is not enough for us, either as married partners or parents. We all need to experience acceptance in order to know that we are loved. Let's take a closer look at what I mean.

Imagine a young boy, Eugene, who has just brought home his report card with good marks. Both mom and dad find it easy to show their acceptance of Eugene's good work. But in the door walks their older daughter, Kathy, who tearfully hands over her report card with — you guessed — some bad marks. How can mom and dad show their concern about her poor grades and at the same time accept their daughter as a worthwhile and competent person? I hope this doesn't seem too hard to do. Here's what the conversation could sound like:

(Kathy walks into the room with her eyes down and a somewhat scared look on her face. She hands her card to her parents, saying): "I feel horrible! Look what I got in science and math!" Mother says: "Well, let's take a look. But, you know before I open this up I want you to know something. I'm more concerned that you're upset. Could we sit down and talk about that first?"

Now this scene could be handled differently. Instead of using words, either mom or dad could simply open their arms and give Kathy a hug and allow her tears to come. Either way, the point I want to make here is that a youngster needs to know love by knowing he is accepted when times are good and when times are bad.

Let's look at six common ways parents can show love and acceptance to their children.

I   First, there is simply telling them, **saying** that you love them. While I stated earlier that this was probably an obvious thing to do on the part of most parents, I want to focus on this way for a moment. It seems to me that our children hear more about how not to do something or how not to act than they hear us tell them how much we love them and appreciate them. While expressing our love may be obvious, it is also obvious that all too often parents forget to express their love and appreciation directly to the child.

II   There is another way besides talking about our love for our children that we can show love and acceptance. This other way is through our gestures and actions — it doesn't involve saying anything. There are several ways within this style of showing our love and acceptance of our children that we will consider. Remember in the earlier scene when Kathy tearfully handed over her report card? I suggested that mom and dad could have held open their arms and given her a hug. That's an example of an action communicating love and acceptance. **Touching is a very powerful way for showing our feelings — especially our feeling of accepting others.** To the preschool child and the early elementary school aged child, brief hugging arms around his shoulder, or gentle stroking of the child's head, holding the child's hand, all communicate love and acceptance. These activities are important because they build a closeness into the parent-child relationship which is needed when times get rougher. Touching is an important and needed experience for the young child. It is as necessary for the parent to provide this contact as it is to provide food and clothing. Now we may do it a little differently at different ages, but touching is important.

III   There is yet another powerful way to share our feelings of acceptance without talking; it may at first sound strange, but it is very real. That way is by staying out of the activities of our children. When we as parents join in our children's activities, there is often an indirect message communicated that goes something like this: "Without me helping you, what you're doing won't go as well." When we allow our children to play or do a project with us being present and watching but not helping we are showing our love and acceptance. What we are showing the child indirectly is: "I accept you and what you do, I am interested in you." In short, by not always playing the part of the master teacher who must show this person what and how to do things, you can show your love and acceptance by giving the child freedom to do it his way. All people, including children, appreciate the freedom to try and fail and to try again. We don't always want help!

Of course, there are times when we must interfer with what our children are doing — when they are endangering themselves or others. But most of the time it is okay to let our children try things out for themselves, even if they aren't doing it exactly the way we would. It is hard for parents to sit back and watch while their children are having trouble. Our natural impulse is to jump in and help. Sometimes they need to struggle with a task, or even fail at it in order to figure out how to do it a better way. We, then, can sometimes best help our children by staying out of their activities.

IV   There is a fourth way of showing our acceptance of our children. It is a kind of return to talking, but not quite. When you hear people talking on the telephone, have you ever noticed how often the following are used: "Uh Huh, Yeah, Hmm, O.K." Or the following: "Tell me more! What then? Can you say more? That's really interesting!" This kind of talking allows the other person to go on and express ideas and feelings, knowing full well he is being heard and accepted. Just like saying, "I love you", or like an accepting touch, or not interfering with what another person is doing, this kind of talking shows acceptance and builds better relationships. We all have known another person who is a good listener and does not interrupt us. The good listener knows how to communicate the brief message: "I am still here and interested in you" by saying things such as "uh huh, and what then?" When a parent is a good listener he builds a relationship with his child and sets the foundation for the sharing of personal feelings and problems as the child grows up.

V.   The fifth way I would like to suggest that can help you communicate your love and acceptance to your child and build your relationship. It may sound, at first, as if I am contradicting what I said earlier about staying out of your children's affairs and activities, but there is an important difference. This last way is by joining in only **some** of your children's activities, but with two basic ground rules that you must follow. First, it is necessary for you to ask to join if you're not already invited. Second, and most importantly, that you take the role of a worker and your child keeps the role of boss of the activity. The differences in this fifth way are clear: you join some of your child's activities and you do not direct those activities once you are involved. In this way you demonstrate that you accept your child by accepting what he's doing. If you start an activity and invite him or he asks to join, then you are the boss. But if he started building a house with blocks, you are the laborer and he is the boss. Let's take a look at some examples of what I've been describing.

Five-year-old Tommy is outside playing with his friends on the slide. Mother is walking by and, as Tommy reaches the top of the steps to slide down, mother yells out: "Be careful Tommy!"

Q. Is the mother in this example showing acceptance of Tommy's activities?

   Pause. Parental response.

Q. How could this mother have shown Tommy love and acceptance in this situation?

   Pause for participants to discuss.

Yes, she could have just stood and watched with a smile on her face, or she could have said, "Boy, does that look like fun."

Now let's examine another example and see if the parents were showing acceptance.

   Six-year-old Jeff was really excited. His grandmother had mailed him a model dinosaur kit and it had just arrived this afternoon. Taking the kit to the basement workshop, Jeff labored over it for hours. Once, when mother went down to put the clothes in the dryer, she noticed he was gluing the head on the tail. Another time, dad went to get a screwdriver, and he saw that the directions for the kit were still in the sealed plastic cover. But neither parent said a thing.

Q. Were mom and dad showing acceptance of Jeff's model building? How did they do it?

   Pause for discussion.

Yes, Jeff didn't ask for help and they let him do the task his way. Now let's return to the first and second examples and change them for a moment.

   This time mother lets Tommy slide and play with his friends without commenting over his every move. Tommy, having played all he wanted, walked over to his mother, who was talking with a neighbor, Jeff's dad. Without stopping her conversation, mother reached down and tousled Tommy's hair and cupped his head in her hand. Shortly, Jeff's dad said I have to go. Jeff's dad then went into the basement workshop and saw, as he expected, Jeff all hunched over the model. Walking over to Jeff he begins picking up the scattered pieces of the model and organizing them. He then says: "I bet these directions could really help! I know they'd help me if I were doing this model. You can't do a job right if you don't follow the directions."

Q. Now what do you think these two parents communicated and how did they do it?

   Pause. Parental response.

Yes, Tommy's mother accepted his behavior and by reaching out and touching him, showed him her affection. Jeff's dad, on the other hand, took over and showed in both actions and words that Jeff wasn't doing things "right." Jeff was told and shown he was unacceptable.

VI There is a sixth way to help build a good parent-child relationship and that is by making frequent use of "helpful praise" and "helpful criticism" which we discussed in our second session. Helpful praise and helpful criticism assists your child in developing positive feelings about himself and we know that we always feel closer to people who help us feel good about ourselves.

   Pause for discussion.

For a moment, let's review the six ways I've suggested that could help a parent build a better relationship with a child.

   Write each category on the board.

First, there is by telling a child you love him. Second, by touching and gestures. Third, by letting a child do his own activities in your presence without taking over. Fourth, there is being the "good listener." Fifth, there is joining with your child in some activities when invited and when you accept the role of workman. Finally, by using helpful praise and helpful criticism.

Now with these in mind again, let's look at the following situation.

Jeannette, full of joy and gladness, announced to mom and dad that she had won a prize in her nursery class. With her face all smiles, she tells how neat it was to win at a game played with her classmates. Now, my question for you is how would you show acceptance of Jeannette regarding this experience? Take a moment and think over the ways I've shared with you. In fact, I'll write the ways on the board. In a moment I would like you to help me make some lists of possible what-to-do's under each of these ways on the board.

Pause for group to think, then collect verbal responses to be written on the board under each of the six headings. (Possible correct responses, e.g., stand there and smile a proud smile, reach out and hug her, say: "Tell me how it went" or "That's neat!"

Now, I would like to add to the story of Jeannette and then see what we can do to show our acceptance. It's now bedtime. Jeannette is being tucked into bed by mom and dad. After fidgeting under the covers for a few minutes, Jeannette finally says: "Mom and Dad, I've got to tell you something. You know the prize I said I won? Well, I didn't win it. See, I found it on the floor in the hall. I knew it was Billy's but I wanted it so much." She begins to cry. "I just put it in my pocket. I just had to tell that story so you would let me keep it."

Q. With this situation, now how would you show acceptance of Jeannette?

Have a three-minute meeting with your neighbor, and then let's make another list under the ways listed on the board.

(Possible constructive response: Mother reaches out and looks at Jeannette with a concerned look. She says, "You are upset by what you did," or "Have you decided what you want to do next?" Pause for three minutes. Then collect listings and discuss them.)

There are a few more examples I would like to share with you. In each of them I would like you to change the situation so that a better relationship will be built by showing acceptance.

After supper, five-year-old Andrew throws himself on the floor in front of the TV. There he lies. Dad can hear Fido whining. He knows that Andrew's dog hasn't been fed yet. This is one of Andy's daily chores. Dad walks by and gives Andy a light kick in the leg and says: "Hey, get your lazy self out there in the kitchen and fix Fido's dish!"

Q. How would you rewrite the script for father's exchange with Andy so that a better relationship could be built?

I would like you to write on a 3 x 5 card what your response would be. Also, write down where that response would best be placed, using those categories on the board.

Pause to allow all to write down their responses.

Now I would like you to hear one more situation. Four-year-old Melissa is busy playing mommy with all her dollies. It's been a lazy Sunday for the rest of the family. Dad, aroused from his nap, goes to look in on Melissa. Looking up as her dad enters the room Melissa says: "Daddy, come play with me and my children. You can be the big brother, but I'm the mommy, OK?

Now, on the back of your 3 x 5 card write down what old dad could do to foster a good relationship with her daughter. Again, decide which of the ways on the blackboard your response fits into best.

Pause for the time for this to be completed.

Having written by this time your two responses, I would like you all to form small groups of three or four people each. For discussion, share with each other what you thought were responses that would help in building good relationships with these children. I will move around and help wherever needed. In ten to fifteen minutes we will have a report from each group telling us your group solutions.

Allow sufficient time for this, probably 10 to 15 minutes.

At this point, I would like to share with you some final thoughts. In this session, I've described some ways that each of you can build better relationships with your children. These ways are geared to let our children know, experience, and feel our love for them. In a sense, these ways are like depositing in a relationship bank account, an account of love and goodwill. We will not at all times be able to deposit; sometimes when we are angry or irritable or busy or needing to discipline our children, we will be withdrawing from our account. If we have a healthy account with our children, those times when we are withdrawing from our relationship account will not lead to a bankrupt relationship with our children. The emphasis, however, needs to be on depositing and not on withdrawing. That's because, like any example I know, it only goes so far in describing truth. In point of fact, the reason we are building relationships with our children is to help them develop into competent and worthwhile people, and this can best be done if a good relationship exists between parent and child.

GENERAL-DISCUSSION   Encourage the parents to share their reactions and feelings about today's session. Encourage application of the ideas to the parent's own family situation, e.g. Mr. Smith seems to see one way this might help his family, can anyone else see how it might work in their family?

6

BUILDING YOUR RELATIONSHIP WITH YOUR CHILD:
PART II—LEARNING TO RECOGNIZE YOUR CHILD'S FEELINGS
THROUGH REFLECTIVE LISTENING

Introduction

Previous lessons have revolved around the need for parents to communicate love and acceptance to their children. Lesson 6 offers one such method of communicating and reflective or active listening (Listening for Feelings).

Haim Ginott (1965) describes a way of conversing with children which he proposed as a way of avoiding "fruitless dialogues" between parents and children (p. 20). These frustrating conversations are the result of parents trying to reason with their children, who resist verbal interchanges because they resent being "preached to, talked at, and criticized." The new method described by Ginott requires that statements of understanding precede statements of advice or instruction. Essentially, he emphasizes the importance of recognizing the feeling behind a child's verbal remarks, and then indicating to the child that these feelings are understood. When the child feels that he has been heard and understood, he is more likely to listen to what his parent has to say.

Ginott's "new method" integrates into the parent-child relationship the same qualities emphasized by Carl Rogers (1957) as helpful in promoting the therapeutic process between a therapist and his client. Rogers' discussions of therapist qualities of empathy, unconditional positive regard and congruence, as well as later research designed to study these qualities (particularly empathy) have definite implications for improving communication between parents and children.

Rogers (1959) defines empathy, or "the state of being empathetic" as (perceiving) the internal frame of reference of another with accuracy and with the emotional components and meanings which pertain thereto as if one were the person...Thus it means to sense the hurt or the pleasure of another as he senses it and to perceive the causes thereof as he perceives them..." (pp. 210-211). More recently Rogers reconceptualized the quality of empathy as a process rather than a state of being (Rogers, 1975). Rogers described the several facets of this process:

"It involves being sensitive, moment to moment, to the changing felt meanings which flow in (the) other person, to the fear or rage or tenderness or confusion or whatever, that he/she is experiencing. It means temporarily living in his/her life, moving about in it delicately without making judgments...It includes communicating your sensings of his/her world...

To be with another in this way means that for the time being you lay aside the views and values you hold for yourself in order to enter another's world without prejudice. In some sense it means that you lay aside yourself and this can only be done by a person who is secure enough in himself that he knows he will not get lost in what may turn out to be the strange or bizarre world of the other, and can comfortably return to his own world when he wishes." (p. 4).

Empathy is a quality which has been singled out as the most important factor in being a therapist. Raskin (1974) studied 83 practicing therapists of approximately 8 different therapeutic approaches. These therapists were in high agreement in giving empathy the highest ranking out of twelve variables when asked to describe their concept of the ideal therapist. This study corroborated an earlier study by Fiedler (1950) who looked at the concept of the "ideal therapy relationship."

Other researchers have found that empathy is correlated with self-exploration and process movement (Bergin and Strupp, 1972; Kurtz and Grummon, 1972). A therapy relationship with a high degree of empathy has been associated with various aspects of process and progress in the therapy, and is particularly related to a high degree of self-exploration in the client. Rogers (1975) describes some of the consequences of the empathetic interaction which he feels contribute to the client's willingness to explore himself and to make changes.

First, empathy dissolves alienation. It helps the therapy client to feel that he has been clearly understood by another human being, and that he is in a positive relationship with that person. Empathetic understanding also lets the recipient know that someone values him, cares for him and accepts him for the person that he is. The message is "this other individual trusts me, thinks I'm worthwhile. Perhaps I *am* worth something. Perhaps I could value *myself.* Perhaps I could care for myself." (Rogers, 1975, p. 7).

Amother impact of empathy comes from its accepting, non-judgmental quality. Rogers feels that this is the highest expression of empahty, for in order to accurately and sensitively understand another person (a client) the therapist must have formed an evaluative opinion. The possibility of self-acceptance by the client is increased as he becomes aware that he is not being judged by the therapist.

Rogers concludes his article with the following statement: "...there are...situations in which the empathetic way of being has the highest priority. When the other person is hurting, confused, troubled, anxious, alienated, terrified; or when he or she is doubtful of self-worth, uncertain as to identity, then understanding is called for. The gentle and sensitive companionship of an empathetic stance — accompanied of course by the other two attitudes (genuineness and caring) — provides illumination and healing. In such situations deep understanding is, I believe, the most gracious gift one can give to another." (1975, p. 9). Although Rogers is addressing himself to the therapy relationship, these words are quite appropriate as a description of the understanding and concern a parent might demonstrate to his child in situations similar to those enumerated. It seems clear that the skill of "reflective listening" — or empathetic listening is an important one for parents to become aware of, and to incorporate in communications with their children. It is helpful as a way of expressing acceptance and understanding to a child, as well as a way of opening pathways of communication.

Thomas Gordon has also incorporated this skill into his ***Parent Effectiveness Program*** (1970). Gordon enumerates several reasons why "active listening" is a helpful skill for parents to learn and also describes a set of basic attitudes a parent must hold in order to use "active listening" effectively. These follow closely along the lines of Rogers' discussions of empathy, particularly regarding the effectiveness of demonstrating empathetic understanding, and the therapist qualities this employs.

The parental attitudes needed in order for "active listening" to be effective are well stated by Gordon (1970, pp. 59-60):

1. The parent must want to hear what the child has to say, and be wiling to take time to listen.
2. The parent must genuinely want to be helpful to the child with the particular problem he presents at a particular time.
3. The parent must be genuinely able to accept the child's feelings, whatever they are, and however different they are from the parent's.
4. The parent must have a deep feeling of trust in the child's capacity to handle his own feelings, and to work toward constructive solutions to his own problems.
5. The parent must appreciate that feelings are transitory and changeable. He must not be afraid of allowing the child to express his feelings.

6. The parent must be able to see the child as someone separate from himself — with his own attitudes, feelings and his own way of perceiving things. The parent should not feel threatened by a child who may not conform to his attitudes, values and beliefs.

CONCLUSIONS: The concept of reflective listening has its foundations in the practice of client-centered psychotherapy, and has been discussed as one method of communication within a parent-child relationship. The specific skill has been incorporated by Ginott and Gordon in their writings in the area of parent education. It has also been introduced here, with some precautions for its use, as a skill that is helpful in developing open and trusting comunication between parents and children. However, it is critical that this skill be viewed as one method that might be incorporated by a parent within a total context of a positive parent-child relationship as described in earlier *Parenting Skills* chapters. It is felt that the use of this "approach" can only be effective if the parent-child relationship already has certain qualities such as warmth, love, mutual concern and sharing, positive regard, etc. to draw from. If these qualities are not present in the relationship, then the approach stands alone with no reinforcement, and is not likely to improve communication between parent and child. In fact, communications might close down if the child preceives the parent to be insincere or phony in "pretending" to show concern or understanding, when there are no other indications of such from the parent's actions.

The method, however, can be a useful one within the context of a "positive" parent-child relationship and is therefore presented in Lesson 6 with opportunities for discussion and practice by group members.

Objectives

1. To sensitize parents to the need to respond to the total communication of their children, including words and feelings.
2. To show parents how to communicate to their children their understanding of their children's feelings.
3. To develop some skill in recognizing feelings implicit in children's communications, and in relating an understanding of these feelings to the child.
4. To help parents understand some of the precautions in using reflective listening ("listening for feelings,").

The skills introduced in this lesson, and the next, are a critical set of skills which must be practiced by the parents, in order to guarantee that they have been satisfactorily acquired. This may require that the trainer insert one or more review and practice session before moving on to any new material. The skills taught in this lesson will be useful to the parents in all subsequent phases of the program, and therefore should be reinforced heavily during this learning phase.

Active roleplaying and parental practice is essential to learning these skills. One of the biggest problems for the trainer is the parents intellectualizing and "talking about" reflective listening, rather than practicing the use of it. Several practice examples, as well as a role-playing activity, have been included to give parents an opportunity to practice. The completion of homework assignments is crucial. The trainer may also encourage the parents' involvement in practicing these new and unfamiliar ways of communicating by the use and modeling of the skills in his interactions with group members.

In teaching the skill of reflective listening, the trainer should point out to the parents that while they may reflect their child's feelings and thereby show the child they understand what is going on inside him, this does not mean they are being permissive, or that they have lowered or altered their standards. For example, if cursing is unacceptable, it remains unacceptable, even though at the time the parent may ignore the cursing and respond to the child's feeling of anger, frustration, etc. The unacceptability of cursing can be discussed at a later time when the child is not in the throes of his emotions — when his feelings have been vented, and he is in a better position to listen to what his parent has to say and work toward a solution of the problem.

While reflective listening can be a very useful tool for parents, there are times when it should not be used. Therefore, the last section of this lesson dealing with the precautions in using reflective listening should be emphasized by the trainer. The basic attitudes required on the part of the parent (as described by Gordon, 1970) are essential to the effective use of the tool. Otherwise, the child will be able to detect the emptiness or insincerity of the parent's remark and communication will break down.

References

1. Bergin, A.E. & Strupp, H.H. *Changing Frontiers in the Science of Psychotherapy.* Chicago: Aldine-Atherton, 1972.

2. Fiedler, F.E. The concept of the ideal therapeutic relationship. *Journal of Consulting Psychology,* 1950, *14,* 239-245.

3. Ginott, H. *Between Parent and Child.* New York: MacMillan Company, 1965.

4. Gordon, T. *Parent Effectiveness Training.* New York: Peter H. Wyden, Inc., 1970.

5. Kurtz, R.R. & Grummon, D.L. Different approaches to the measurement of therapist empathy and their relationship to therapy outcomes. *Journal of Consulting and Clinical Psychology,* 1972, *39,* 106-115.

6. Raskin, N. Studies on psychotherapeutic orientation: Idealogy in practice. *AAP Psychotherapy Research Monographs.* Orlando, Florida: American Academy of Psychotherapists, 1974.

7. Rogers, C.R. The necessary and sufficient conditions of therapeutic personality change. *Journal of Consulting Psychology,* 1957, *21,* 95-103.

8. Rogers, C.R. A theory of therapy, personality, and interpersonal relationships as developed in the client-centered framework. In S. Koch (Ed.) *Psychology: A Study of a Science, Vol. III.* New York: McGraw-Hill, 1959, 184-256.

9. Rogers, C.R. Empathetic: An Unappreciated Way of Being. *The Counseling Psychologist,* 1975, *5* (2), 2-10.

Materials

1. Movable chairs   2. Blackboard

Reference

Gordon, Thomas, *Parent Effectiveness Training.* New York: Peter H. Wyden, 1970, Chapters 3-5.

Sequence

1. Review and sharing of home practice (20-30 minutes)
2. Lecture-discussion (30 minutes)
3. General discussion (20-30 minutes)

REVIEW AND SHARING OF HOME PRACTICE   Last week we discussed four different ways of communicating love and acceptance and we had a home practice assignment to practice using these different ways.

Q. Would someone be willing to share a description of a situation in which they used one of the four ways to communicate love and acceptance to their child?

You must be very reinforcing to the volunteer, and you should encourage him and then the others in the workshop to consider other good ways of communicating love and acceptance to their child?

LECTURE-DISCUSSION   In this session I'm going to suggest some ways that you can definitely improve how you communicate with a child. These are ways that will work for everyone with just a little practice. I believe that all of us, as parents, want to have a good relationship with our children and we want them to love us. I believe it's just as sure that our children also want to love us and feel close to us. When we have a good relationship with our children, we will help them believe that they are lovable, worthwhile, competent, and responsible. During this session I am going to show you how you can do two things to build a better relationship and communicate love to your child.

First is how to recognize what your child feels. Second is how to let your child know you understand his feelings by communicating them to him.

If we all think about it for a minute, we will realize that children express their feelings in many ways. Sometimes it's in plain words like, "Mommy, I love you," or "You're mean, I don't like you."

These words are easy to understand. No problem here! But, sometimes children send us their feelings in words that need figuring out.

For Example:

1. It's Saturday afternoon and Billy, age four, says to his father in a mildly pleading tone of voice: "Are you going to work all day, daddy?"

2. Sally, age six, asks her mother about her three-month-old sister. In a mildly angry tone of voice she asks: "Why do you let that nosiy old baby sleep in your room?"

These words don't quite tell us as clearly as those used in the other examples. Here we have to listen not to just the words, but also the tone of voice and when it is said. We can see that Billy wanted his father to play with him, and Sally was expressing her feeling of being left out.

Here is another way that children let us know how they are feeling.

Belinda Sue is sent to her room for misbehaving; she doesn't have to say she is mad. We can see her frown and the way she storms up the stairs. We can also hear the door slam.

When Frank, Jr. comes home from school and goes straight to his room and doesn't say "Hi," like he usually does, we know something is wrong.

These examples show us that understanding the feelings of a child is like listening to a song — you have to pay attention to the music as well as the words. When you look at your child's expression, watch his gestures and listen to his tone of voice in addition to listening to words, you will then recognize his feelings.

Now, if we learn to recognize our children's feelings but do nothing with this recognition, then we are wasting the material out of which a close relationship is built. When someone recognizes our feelings and lets us know that they understand, that is what pulls us closer together. When a friend recognizes that you are upset and says, "Jim you seem a little upset today," he has shown you that he notices and to some degree cares about how you feel. If he has good sense and doesn't say any more, then he gives you the opportunity to share your concern or problem if you want, and that sharing will bring you closer together.

Now if we don't listen for our children's feelings we can have two bad things happen. First, we miss a chance to build our relationship and to communicate love and acceptance to our child. Second, we are likely not to understand our child's communication and to turn him or her off to seeing his parents as a source of help and understanding. I am going to give you some examples of bad parent-child communication so that you can see why many children, particularly teenagers, don't talk to their parents and wouldn't come to them for help.

1. Child (dejected tone of voice): "I don't think I want to go to chorus anymore."
   Parent (firmly with annoyance): "Let's not have any of that stuff. You will go to chorus."

2. Child (angrily): "That Sarah is a rotten bitch."
   Parent (annoyed and angry): "Listen here, young lady, don't you ever let me hear you talk like that again."

3. Child (pleading): "Mom, do I have to do it now?"
   Parent (annoyed and angry): "Patrick, do your chores, do you hear me?"

It is easy to see that each of these replies by the parent is a sure bet not to improve the parent-child relationship. Each response threatens the use of parental power. Each in its own way tells the child that he is not worthwhile. In short, the message is you shouldn't talk like that, I cannot accept you. Let's look at the same examples again, but this time there will be different sets of responses, which are helpful.

1. Child (dejected tone of voice): "I don't think I want to go to chorus anymore."
   Parent (concerned): "Jim, you sure sound unhappy."
2. Child (angrily): "That Sarah is a rotten bitch."
   Parent (concerned): "Sometimes she gets you really angry."
3. Child (pleading tone of voice): "Mom, do I have to do it now?"
   Parent (firmly): "You would like to something else?"

Now, together let's try to recognize the ways that hinder and the ways that help in talking to our children. Remember, using power is destructive in building relationships, and so is giving away power because it is too permissive. Rather, our goal is to understand and to share our understanding of our children's feelings. In this last way, our sons and daughters will know that mom and dad accept them and respect them.

I'm going to relate some conversations between parents and children, but in each situation I'll give three possible parental replies. You are to choose which one is based on power, which one is based on permissiveness, and which one is based on recognition of the child's feelings.

> *Child: "Gosh, Mom, we aren't having asparagus again, are we?"*
> *Parent 1: "You don't have to eat it."*
> *Parent 2: "It sounds like you don't like the vegetable?"*
> *Parent 3: "Stop your griping."*

Q. O.K. Who would like to identify which reply was the one that used power;

> *Pause for answer*

Q. Which one used permissiveness?

> *Pause for answer.*

Q. Which one used listening for feeling?

> *Pause for answer.*

I'm glad to see that we are getting the idea. Let's try another one.

> *Child (longingly): "Will Daddy be home soon?"*
> *Parent 1: "You miss him."*
> *Parent 2: "Stop pestering. When he gets home, he'll be home."*
> *Parent 3: "Why don't you call him and ask him to come home soon."*

Again, ask for responses that identify use of power, permissiveness, and reflecting feeling.

Extra examples for use if needed.

> *Child (angrily): "I hate school and I'm not going tomorrow."*
> *Parent 1: "Don't say things like that. It can't be that bad."*
> *Parent 2: "It sounds like you had a bad day at school."*
> *Parent 3: "If it's that important to you, you can stay home tomorrow."*

> *Child (crying): "Mommy, Jane's being mean to me. She took my crayons away."*
> *Parent 1: "Jane, give Lucy her crayons. You should know better than to take things from your little sister."*
> *Parent 2: "Jane took your crayons and you're unhappy and angry with her."*
> *Parent 3: "Lucy, if you'll stop crying, maybe I can understand what you're saying."*

Child (excitedly): "I've been wishing our scout troup would go camping, and now we're going. I can't wait!"
Parent 1: "I'm so glad. You sound really excited about the trip!"
Parent 2: "We'll have to ask your Dad if it will be all right for you to go."
Parent 3: "That's nice. I'll help you start packing."

Child (frustrated): "Dad, this homework is dumb. It's too hard. Can you help me?"
Parent 1: "Sorry, but I'm watching the news right now. Keep trying and I'll help in a while."
Parent 2: "Sure, I can help. Let's see what the problem is!"
Parent 3: "You sound pretty frustrated. That must be a tough homework assignment. I'll be with you after the news."

Child (proudly): "Mom, we got report cards today and I didn't make any C's. Aren't you proud of me?"
Parent 1: "Yes! And you seem to be happy about it, too."
Parent 2: "See, I told you that hard work would pay off."
Parent 3: "Of course I'm proud of you. Let's have an ice cream cone to celebrate."

(Argument between parent and child regarding going to another child's house.)

Child: "I hate you. You never let me do anything!"
Parent 1: "Well, if you're going to act like that, I'd rather you go to John's. Go ahead."
Parent 2: "You are angry at me. But I cannot agree to you going to John's house when his parents aren't home."
Parent 3: "Don't talk back to me. I said no, and that's final!"

I can see right now that you are beginning to see the differences between these three responses. We are now on our way to learning how to talk effectively to children by listening for our children's feelings. I would like to point out that you could have responded to each of these two children's statements by answering what they said rather than how they said it. For example, a parent could have responded to the children with a "yes" or "no" regarding both the asparagus and daddy's arrival. But if this occurred, only a portion of the child's talking would have been heard. To hear the melody is also to hear the feelings, and that's what we are trying to learn to do in this session.

Maybe I need to clarify this difference a little more. A child does not always need to have his own feelings communicated to him, especially when he wants only information. Those times in which reflecting feeling is most helpful is when more than just information is needed. What is also needed is acceptance and understanding of the child' feelings. For example, if a child says: "Well, I'm leaving for school now," it would be silly to say, "You feel like leaving now." But if a child whines, saying, "I just don't like that dumb old school. Why do I have to go?" then more than information is being asked and needed. This is one time to listen to your child's feelings and communicate that you understand them.

Let's try situations in which listening for feelings would help build a better relationship. I'll give you some conversations in which the parent either uses power or permissiveness and I would like you to correct the parental response by giving a reply, which shows you are listening for feelings.

Child: "Will I always wake up when I go to sleep?"
Parent: "Don't be silly, you baby, of course you wake up after sleeping."

Q. Now this parent has, with power, missed not only the bullseye, but the whole target. What could he have said that would have demonstrated that the child's feelings were understood?

Pause for possible answers. Try to get several different ones.

O.K. Those were good. The bullseye has been hit when you show understanding of not only the words, but also the fellings. Let's try another one.

> **Child (anxiously): "I didn't want to go in the swimming pool. It's too cold and I don't like the water."**
> **Parent: "You don't have to go in if you don't want to."**

Here the permissive parent has also missed the target.

Q. Why did this parent miss the target? What are some listening for feelings statements you could make to this child that would be right on target?

> *Pause and collect several possible statements. Summarize. (The parent should reflect the child's concern and fears.)*

I feel like we're ready to try some more listening for feelings. This time, I'll give each of you an opening message as though I were the child. When I'm done, you are to communicate to me what you think I feel. If it's not quite on target, I'll try to come back again with another version of the same message. If you are right on the button, I'll tell you right away. In this way, each of us will have a chance to try our solo wings in listening for feelings.

> *Ask for volunteers, but indicate that all will be asked to try an example. Prompt parents by giving them the initial part of their responses: "I bet you are feeling _____." or "You seem to be very _____." Use the prompt for the first 2-3 examples. For the following examples, pause for parent response, and use prompts when needed. For training purposes it is more important for the parent to indicate that he understands the feeling being expressed in this exercise, then to be able to converse with the child.*

1. Angry and indignant): "Boy, do I hate my new teacher. She's so crabby. She's too strict."
   (Response: "You're angry at your new teacher.")
2. (Pleading): "I don't want to eat these baked potatoes. I hate them."
   (Response: "You don't like potatoes.")
3. (Pleading and forlorn): "I don't have anything to do today. What can I do? I wish there was something to do!"
   (Response: "You're bored and lonely.")
4. (Angry and confused): "I hate Julie. She always cries and tries to get her way. If I don't do what she wants, she goes home."
   (Response: "You're angry and confused.")
5. (Stubborn and indignant): "I don't want to take a bath. I'm not even dirty. I hate baths anyway. Why do I have to take a bath every day anyway?"
   (Response: "You don't want to take a bath.")
6. (Tearfully): "Fran won't let me play with her dolls. She's mean. Make her give me some of them to play with."
   (Response: "You're angry with Fran.")
7. (Child hurts finger with hammer): "Ow! Ow! It hurts! Sob. Ow!"
   (Response: "It sure hurts!")
8. (Pleading): "I want to sleep in your room. I don't like to sleep in my old room. Can I sleep with you and daddy?"
   (Response: "You're lonely in your room.")
9. (Pleading and annoyed): "Times have changed since you were a kid. You're old-fashioned. All the girls my age wear lipstick now."
   (Response: "You want to the things the other girls do so you won't be left out.")
10. (Tearfully): All the other girls are having dates except me. What is the matter with me? Why don't I get asked for dates?"
    (Response: "You feel left out and lonely.")

11. (Confused): "I don't know what to do. Part of me wants to do nothing, but part of me wants to do something."
   (Response: "You're confused.")
12. (Angrily): "I'm not going to clean up my room. I hate to clean it up. It's my room and I'm going to keep it the way I want to."
   (Response: "You don't want to be told what to do.")
13. (Initially matter-of-factly, becomes more dramatic): "I don't want my dinner tonight. I'm not hungry. Just don't serve me anything. I just couldn't eat anything tonight, the way I feel about things."
   (Response: "You're upset.")
14. (Angered): "I wish I weren't a kid. I'll sure be glad when I'm grown up. It's no fun being a kid."
   (Response: "You're unhappy and you're upset.")

Now, some of you probalby felt that it's not always easy to get in touch with the feeling of these children's messages. I would urge you to realize that it is practice that will make you feel more comfortable. While reflective listening may seem strange at first, I have found that parents learn very quickly. The reason is simple. When you see your child's eyes brighten when he really knows you understand him, you will be rewarded so fully that you'll find yourself working to use this skill more and more. And that's the beauty of this skill — it builds better relations with our children quickly and positively.

We know that the closer the parent-child relationship, the less often high-power techniques, such as spanking, are needed in discipline. The closeness of the parent-child relationship builds the child's belief that he is a lovable and worthwhile person and that he is respected as a competent and responsible individual. Listening for your child's feelings and letting him know you understand by reflecting them back are important skills worth working on.

PRACTICE EXERCISE FOR LISTENING FOR FEELINGS SKILLS   Divide the group into triads. The parents within these triads will take turns as child, parent, and observer. Pass out cards (one set for each triad) with the description of the situation and the child's statement. Have the "child" read the card and allow "parent" to respond. They should then continue the conversation for 2-3 minutes. The person who is observing should provide "parent" with feedback as to appropriateness of the responses given. The group leader should move among triads providing encouragement and feedback.

SPECIFIC DIRECTIONS TO THE TRIADS   We are going to do some role playing with each of you taking turns being a parent, a child and an observer. This is how our groups will work. First, the person who is the "child" will read the card to set the scene and start the conversation. The "parent" will respond to the "child" with a statement which shows "listening for feelings." Then continue the conversation for 2-3 minutes, with the "parent" using a "listening for feeling" statement at least one more time. The observer needs to pay close attention so that he can point out any other occasions when a "listening for feeling" statement would have been appropriate. The "child" should pay close attention to what the "parent" says to him, so that he can tell the "parent" what his reactions were during their conversation. Think about how you felt, what you thought, how you wanted to respond.

Each person should get 4 cards. You will be the "child" for those 4 role-plays. The other two people should take turns being the parent or the observer, that means 2 times as parent and twice as observer. When you've finished one group of cards, someone else will become the child, and the others will become parent and observer. Keep going around until all your cards have been used. Any questions?

EXAMPLES FOR GROUP EXERCISE: (These should be printed on 3x5 index cards to be passed out to the triads).

1. Five-year-old Mary has just come in from playing outside. She is crying, and says to her mommy:
   "Mommy, I don't like Sue anymore. She won't play with me in my store. She wants to play dolls with Nancy."
2. Terry is working his model car as his Dad walks into the room. Terry says (excitedly):
   "Dad, look how I fixed my car! Doesn't it look great with the decals?"
3. Martha, who is three, begins to cry when Mommy and Daddy are leaving to go out for the evening. The babysitter tries very hard to console her, but Martha just cries louder. She then reaches up to her mommy and says:
   "Martha go, too."
4. John, who is thirteen, has just come home with a test paper that he failed. He says:
   "I'm just going to quit school. I can't pass Mr. Smith's tests no matter how hard I study. I'm just no good at anything."
5. Mark, age 7, calls excitedly to his mother:
   "Mom, Dad said we can go skating Saturday. I wish it was Saturday already!"
6. Christy, age 6, has just started school. Her mother is having a difficult time getting Christy ready to go on her 4th day. Christy says to her mother (pleading & stubbornly):
   "I don't want to go to school today. I want to stay here with you and play with my puppy."
7. Beth, age 15, has been asked to 2 different parties on the same night. She comes to her mother and asks:
   "Mom, I don't know what to do now. Should I go to Jane's party or to Tom's party?"
8. Jeff, age 12, wants to go on a weekend camping trip with his friends. His father had to tell him that he couldn't go because Jeff would miss his mother's birthday party. Jeff says (angrily):
   "Why do I have to be at the party? I never get to do what I want to do!"
9. Susie's mother is in the hospital, waiting to come home with a new baby. Susie says to her father one night at bedtime:
   "When is mommy coming home. I want **her** to read my book."
10. Mike, age 10, has been trying hard to finish cleaning up his room so that he can go out and play. His mother comes in to see how he is doing, but he is only half finished. Mike says (pleading):
    "Can't I go out to play now? I really have been working hard. See how neat my bed is?"
11. Angela, age 9, wants to play ball with her older brother Jim, who is 13. Angela comes to her father and says:
    "I want to play, too, but Jim won't let me. He just laughs when I ask him, and says I'm not big enough. Make him let me play, okay?"
12. Steve, age 8, watches as his mother is rocking his new baby sister. He walks over to the chair, smiles at the baby and leans over to kiss her. Steve says to his mother:
    "I want to rock my baby, too. Can I please hold her?"

Before we stop this session, there are some rules of caution that you must follow in using these skills. When you hear your child's feelings and reflect them back to him to show your understanding, you are signaling him to talk more and go on expressing himself.

However, there are times and conditions under which you shouldn't signal your child to continue talking and expressing his feelings. These will be explained more fully below. It has been found that under certain conditions, the practice of listening for your child's feelings may lead to more conflict or may stand in the way of building a good parent-child relationship. There are times when listening for feelings is not helpful. While we cannot predict every situation in which the practice of listening for feelings may have a negative effect on the parent-child relationship, the following are common circumstances where it might. You should not use "listening for feelings" in these situations.

1. Don't listen for your child's feelings if the feelings he is expressing are ones you cannot accept, or feel are wrong. For example, Mrs. Jones is a very sensitive person, and her 7-year-old son says to her, "I hate you. You're mean." Since this is very likely to upset Mrs. Jones, she needs to examine her own feelings and reactions first. Once she can understand her own feelings, she will be in a better position to help her child explore his feelings.

2. Don't respond to your child by listening to his feelings if you do not have time to let your child express himself fully. For example, you are about to leave the house, and want to be on time for an appointment, and your daughter says: "Mom, I don't want to stay with the babysitter again today." By responding, "You're unhappy because I need to leave you again," you leave the door open for more conversation. Since you don't have the time to talk you may cut your child off abruptly, after signaling her to talk with a "listening for feelings" response, and she will feel more unhappy than before.

3. Don't listen for feelings if you cannot help at that particular time. If you are occupied or too busy to stop and help your child when he asks for it, you should not lead your child to think that you have the time to by responding with a listening for feeling statement. Rather than cutting him off before he has expressed himself fully, it would be better to wait until later, or until the next time he asks.

4. If you are not willing to work on your feelings of trust toward your child's proposed solutions to his problems, don't encourage him to talk about them by listening for feelings. If you do not feel that your child is able to make decisions for himself, you may let him talk about his solutions, then put him down by giving him your solution. He will then start feeling that you're not really interested in what he has to say, because when he's finished, you'll tell him what to do anyway. He will soon begin to think that he is not a worthwhile or competent person.

5. You don't want to listen to your child's feelings, if you do not see him as a separate person with the right to develop his own feelings. As a separate person, your child is entitled to disagree with you or to think you are wrong or even foolish at times. However, you may not think that your child should disagree with his parents. For example, you daughter or son may feel very strongly that you are unfair because you will not allow him/her to stay overnight at a friend's house when their parents aren't home. If you are not prepared to hear his objections to your decision, or do not think he should be allowed to disagree, do not say that you understand he is angry and thereby encourage him to express his anger. You should not encourage him to talk about something you will not be willing to listen to. The situation would then become more frustrating for you and your child.

When you are in a situation with your child, and are trying to decide whether to respond by listening to his feelings, ask yourself these questions:

Q. Am I willing to allow him to express these feelings, and talk them out?

or

Q. Will I put him down, or cut him short, because I can't accept what he will say?"

If the answer to the second question is "yes," don't use listening for feelings.

GENERAL DISCUSSION

Q. Can anyone see how they might apply the ideas presented in this session to their family situation?

Encourage application of the ideas presented to the parents' family situation.

7

BUILDING YOUR RELATIONSHIP WITH YOUR CHILD:
PART III — SHARING YOURSELF

Introduction

A great deal has been said in previous lessons about listening to and responding to children. Several skills have been introduced as techniques for facilitating communication with children and for encouraging children to communicate openly with their parents. While this is certainly a significant aspect of child rearing, it is just as important that parents communicate openly with their children about their feelings and ideas, in such a way that children learn to listen to and accept their parents. This is the second part of building open, loving, and respectful relationships between parents and children.

The counseling and psychotherapy literature provides a basis for the "sharing yourself" skill introduced in Lesson 7. Rogers (1957) mentions "congruence" or "genuineness" as one of three therapist qualities he feels are essential to the establishment of an effective client-therapist relationship. He defines congruence as the act of being transparent, that is, hiding nothing of one's experience in a relationship. Rogers feels that the therapist, by being himself freely and openly, is offering the possibility of an existential encounter between two real persons, and thus creates a therapeutic atmosphere within the relationship. In later works, Rogers (1961, 1975) states that in ordinary interactions of life — between marital partners, parent and child, teacher and student, or between colleagues, it is probable that congruence is the most important element. This genuineness involves the personally owned and straightforward expression of both negative and positive feelings. Congruence is thus a basis for living together in an atmosphere of intimacy and realness, according to Rogers.

Jourard (1971a, 1971b) has theorized about and has done extensive research in the area of "self-disclosure," or the act of fully, spontaneously and honestly revealing one's self (attitudes, feelings, thoughts, beliefs) to another person. An important finding of Jourard's research is that self-disclosure from another increased self-disclosure between individuals in a relationship and increased the sense of closeness. Sarason, et al. (1972) concluded that self-disclosure by a model modified the tendency of defensive persons to avoid dealing with emotions, conflicts, and disturbing thoughts. Stone and Gottlib (1975) also found that modeling of self-disclosure facilitated self-disclosing behavior in male students. The results of these various studies have definite implications for parents who wish to have close, loving relationships with their children.

It seems clear that the act of making one's feelings, attitudes, beliefs and thoughts known in an honest, straightforward manner is important in developing an intimate, trusting relationship with another person. It is also clear that self-disclosure, or genuineness, can be fostered in others through modeling. Therefore, self-disclosing parents are likely to facilitate patterns of communication with their children in which both negative and positive feelings, opinions, etc. can be expressed freely in a climate of mutual love and respect.

Gordon (1970) discussed self-disclosure as a way of insuring that a parent's needs and rights will be accounted for without berating his child's feelings and wishes. He introduces the techniques of the "I-message" for use in situations where a parent feels that his needs are being violated, and he wants to confront the child in order to work out a mutually satisfying solution. Gordon indicates several reasons why he believes "I-messages" are effective:

1. Communicating openly to a child the effect of his behavior on the parent is less threatening, and therefore less apt to provoke resistance and rebellion.
2. The child is given responsibility for his behavior, and allowed an opportunity for doing something about it.
3. The parent, by honestly communicating his feelings, influences the child to express his feelings whenever he has them. This flow of honest communication fosters an intimate, interpersonal relationship between the parent and child, where both share an attitude of trust and acceptance for each other.

Gordon seems to present this technique as an intervention strategy for parent-child conflicts. The **Parenting Skills** program introduces the use of "sharing yourself" statements as a skill to be learned by parents as one way of facilitating intimate, interpersonal interactions with children. It is presented as a means for building a positive parent-child relationship, rather than an intervention technique, and therefore differs from Gordon's use of the "I-message." Both strategies are practical applications of the notions related to "congruence" and "self-disclosure" which have been presented above.

References

1. Gordon, T. *Parent Effectiveness Training.* New York: Peter W. Wyden, 1970.
2. Jourard, S.M. *Self-Disclosure: An Experimental Analysis of the Transparent Self.* New York: John Wiley & Sons, 1971a.
3. Jourard, S.M. *The Transparent Self.* New York: D. Van Nostrand Company, 1971b.
4. Rogers, C.R. The necessary and sufficient conditions of therapeutic personality change. *Journal of Consulting Psychology,* 1957, *21,* 95-103.
5. Rogers, C.R. *On Becoming a Person.* Boston: Houghton Mifflin, 1961.
6. Rogers, C.R. Empathetic: An unappreciated way of being. *The Counseling Psychologist,* 1975, *5* (2), 2-10.
7. Sarason, I.Q., Ganzer, V. and Singer, M. Effects of modeled self-disclosure on the verbal behavior of persons differing in defensiveness. *Journal of Consulting & Clinical Psychology,* 1972, *39,* 483-490.
8. Stone, G. and Gottlib. Effect of instructions and modeling on self-disclosure. *Journal of Counseling Psychology,* 1975, *22* (4), 288-293.

Objectives

1. To help parents build their relationships with their children by sharing their feelings and ideas with them in constructive ways.
2. To help parents recognize communications with their children which are destructive to the parent-child relationship.
3. To help set reasonable expectations of parents for themselves in terms of sharing their own feelings.

Special Notes for Trainers

As in the previous lesson, the practice of the skills presented here is paramount. Parents are probably not used to the idea that it is all right to express *their* feelings, and therefore need to engage in this activity until they feel comfortable communicating in this manner. Participation in the exercises provided in the lesson and the completion of homework assignments are essential in learning this skill. The trainer may again want to spend an extra session devoted to practice and role-playing activities before proceeding to new material. Also the trainer can encourage the use of "sharing yourself" statements, and ease parental anxiety and uncomfortableness by sharing his own thoughts and feelings in a constructive way as he interacts with group members.

It is important that the trainer not mislead parents to believe that this skill is an intervention strategy to use when communication has broken down, or during other times of conflict. This skill is a relationship-building strategy, rather than a panacea for avoiding or solving conflicts within a parent-child relationship. If used consistently and appropriately within the context of fostering honest, interpersonal interactions between parent and child, this approach can be very effective. However, the use of such an approach in the communications between a parent and a child, who do not have a particularly positive relationship, may result in frustration and hurt feelings on the part of the parent and/or the child. The trainer is therefore advised to have the parents use "positive sharing yourself" statements as they begin to practice this skill with their own children. Parents must be made aware that their children may not respond to, or may ignore their sharing statements. If negative feelings (such as unhappiness, hurt, exasperation, anger) have been shared and there has been no response from the child, this parent may become resistant to the use of the "sharing yourself" communications.

The discussion period following the formal presentation and role-playing activity should be used to discuss the parents' reactions to expressing their feelings to children. It is particularly helpful to discuss the vulnerability of the parent in those situations when he shares himself, and the threat of feeling ignored, rejected, or put-down. A discussion of negative self-talks, such as "If my child doesn't react favorably when I tell him how I feel, then he doesn't care about my feelings," would be quite appropriate at this point (the trainer may want to refer ahead in the Training Manual to those lessons dealing with self-talks, in order to introduce the topic here). This is also an excellent opportunity to reemphasize the importance of "reflective listening" in helping a child to feel heard and understood. During the course of Lesson 7, the parents are able to experience the sharing of feelings, in the same way that their children did during Lesson 6. They can now discuss, from their new vantage point, the virtues of using "listening for feeling" statements in their communications with their children.

Materials

1. Blackboard, chalk, and eraser
2. Movable chairs arranged in a circle

Sequence

1. Review and sharing of home practice (20-30 minutes)
2. Lecture-discussion (30-40 minutes)
3. General discussion (20-30 minutes)

REVIEW AND SHARING OF HOME PRACTICE   Last week we learned about the importance of recognizing your child's feelings as a way of building a closer and strong parent-child relationship. Would someone be willing to share the results of their home practice assignment with the rest of us?

LECTURE-DISCUSSION   For a moment I want to remind us all that the things we will learn in this session as well as the things we learned about in the last couple of sessions are designed to help build good close relationships with our children. Our goal, remember, is to help our children believe in and experience themselves as being worthwhile and competent. When we communicate love and acceptance, we demonstrate to our children, and encourage them to respect themselves and believe in themselves. The same is true when we use reflective listening to show them that we recognize their feelings.

Now, there is still another way to build a closer relationship with your child. That other way is what I want to share with you in this session. What is this other way? Simply put, it is sharing yourself with your children. Now what does that mean? It means letting your children know and experience your thoughts and feelings. Do you remember the session on Evaluating the Parent-Child Relationship? In that session one of the things we talked about was knowing the signs that identify difficulties between parents and children. One of these signs was when the parent used destructive communication. Now, in destructive communication, parents do communicate their thoughts and feelings, but these will not build better relationships with our children.

Let's consider some common destructive communications between parents and children. One of the most common factors in destructive communication is the parent solving a problem the child is having by telling him a solution. We all know that children cannot solve all problems without help, and parents will sometimes need to give the child some information. The destructiveness in communicating solutions to children (and others) is the hidden message that says: "you are not competent enough to deal with this problem without my help." If the parent is almost always telling his child solutions, then his commuinication will be destructive and, in the long run, will damage the child's sense of competence, and the parent-child relationship. Let's consider some examples of the unnecessary destructive communication of sending solutions.

> *Jimmy, age four, is slowly picking up his toys and blocks and putting them away. This job is going slowly since Jimmy tried to carry as much as possible in each trip and drops half or more of the toys and blocks on the way. His father says: "Jimmy, if you carry less, you can get it done faster. You could make more trips and you wouldn't have to keep stopping to pick up the things you drop."*
>
> *"Susie! If you want your sand castle to stand, you must build it farther from the ocean."*
>
> *"Jeffrey, if you call each of the neighbors, maybe one of them would have a sleeping bag you could borrow."*

Each of these examples represents a situation in which either the child can be expected to find the solution or the situation will teach it to him. He will learn from the consequences of his behavior. He doesn't need a solution from his parent.

The second common factor of destructive communication involves the use of the word "you". If we want to share ourselves with our children, if we want to build closer relationships, then we must understand the destructiveness of communicating to our children by using sentences that involve the word "you". Let me give you some examples of such sentences.

1. "John, you are being a bad boy. You shouldn't pull on people's clothing; stop it or I will slap you."
2. "Billy, you are making too much noise. Stop it."
3. "Carol, you are making me mad. Go to your room."
4. "Jane, you are being selfish if you don't share the candy."

In each of these examples, the child is being blamed and judged, yet he may not know exactly why. He is also being given a solution. Now, sometimes, this kind of communication is useful to the parent since it solves the immediate problem. However, in this session, we are talking about building a closer relationship with our children, and we know that communications involving "you" statements and solutions don't help build the parent-child relationship. They are, in fact, a drain on the relationship. When parents tell their child something in a "you," sentence, they are kind of drawing a line between "you" the child, and "I" the parent. We all know that closeness involves sharing and being on the same side.

Let's see if we cannot handle the problem of communicating to our children in a more constructive way. First, we must recognize that the parent may often have strong feelings and emotions that need to be expressed. The parent's feelings, ideas, values, expectations, and standards are important and should be communicated to children. The problem becomes how to do this so that it builds a closer relationship between parent and child.

Let me go back to the four original examples of destructive communication and restate them in a constructive way designed to build the parent-child relationship through "sharing yourself."

1. "John, I am very busy and worried now and I can't pay attention to you like I would like to."
2. "Billy, I am working on my checkbook and I need quiet so I won't make a mistake."
3. "Carol, I get very upset when I see my children hurt each other. I love you all and I get sad when I see anyone hurt."
4. "Jane, I bought the candy for all of my family because I know everyone likes it. If it is not shared, I will be disappointed."

Now, what is the difference between these two ways of talking to our children?

Pause. Wait for parental responses and write them on blackboard.

We can all see that the second way of talking to children is more personal. We are sharing our feelings, ideas, expectations, and standards, and that helps build a closer parent-child relationship and that's good. You will also note that the sentences included the word "I" as opposed to the word "you."

Write "I" and "you" on the blackboard.

Sentences which start with "I" and don't include "you" tell about the feelings, ideas, values, and expectations of the speaker. The person who uses sentences starting with "I" and that don't include "you" is sharing himself! This person is opening up his private world to other people. He is saying, I want you to know me, to be close to me. In a way, this person is saying, you are somebody special.

You will also note that "sharing yourself" statements don't involve sending solutions; there is no advising, warning, counseling, or putting responsibility or blame on the other person. The receiver of the message hears directly what you think and feel, and he still has all the choices to do whatever he wants.

This way of talking also has the effect of communicating the parent's trust, respect, and belief in his child. We must also realize that if we don't have a strong relationship with our child, he may just ignore our feelings, ideas, values, and expectations, and that is one of the dangers and risks of this kind of communication. We could find out that we don't have a good relationship with our child and he or she will ignore our feelings and needs and continue doing whatever it was that concerned us. Therefore, you must remember that whenever you are "sharing yourself," you must not think of it as a way of controlling your child.

"Sharing yourself" is a method of building a better relationship and we know that people with close relationships will take into consideration the feelings, ideas, values, and expectations of people they love and feel close to. "Sharing yourself" is a way in which close families influence the behavior of each other, but the object of the method is developing closeness, understanding, and love, not power, over one another.

Now there are times when parents use a false "I" in their attempts to "share themselves." This happens when the message starts with "I," but involves the two parts of destructive messages mentioned earlier, namely, the sending of solutions or some blaming or judgment of the child. It is important that you learn the difference between phony and disguised destructive messages and real "sharing yourself" messages:

"I feel frustrated when you behave so stupidly."
"I feel good when you do your good samaritan bit."
"I am angry when you don't keep your promises. Nobody will be able to trust you."
"I am tired of your sloppiness."

In each of these there is a sense of "I feel" from the sender, but the net result is that name-calling sarcasm, and solution-sending are also present. The form of "sharing yourself" is there, but not the spirit.

We have now identified three different kinds of communication that will effect the closeness of your relationship to your child.

Write on blackboard the three headings as follows: Describe each as you write them.

Destructive method
  a) blaming, judging, ridicule
  b) solution sending

Phony sharing yourself
  a) using "I" format
  b) blaming, judging, ridicule
  c) solution sending

Sharing yourself
  a) using yourself "I" as starting point
  b) genuine expression of feelings, values, expectations

I am going to tell you two stories and I would like you to decide, using the chart on the blackboard as a guide, what kind of message each character is sending.

It's been a long week and a hard day for Mr. and Mrs. Brown. Supper is over and everyone is relaxed in the living room watching TV. Even grandma stopped by to drop off some cookies. The phone rings. Timmy's kindergarten teacher tells Mr. Brown that Timmy was cursing in school. After the call, Mr. Brown tells Timmy and the whole house what his teacher said. Then each person says something to Timmy.

Dad: "When I hear these stories from your teacher I get angry and disappointed when you behave like a lousy, rotten kid. I could break your neck."

Mom: "Timmy, dear, you really ought to know better. You can see how you upset your father and the whole family."

Grandmother: "I feel disappointed and kind of sad. I have a lot of pride in my grandchildren. I wonder what happened in school?"

Given what was said, with which grown-up will Timmy probably feel closest? Can you identify which grown-up is using which of these communication styles?

Take a few minutes for the participants to answer and discuss their impressions.

So far, so good. Let's try another one.

Rosemary, a six-year-old, is playing with her toys in the living room. Before long, they are scattered all over the place. It is getting near supper time, and her Daddy will soon be home from work. Mother wants to have the living room straightened up some so Daddy can at least find his way to his chair. Mother asks young Rosemary to please clean up her toys. Rosemary says okay, yet fifteen minutes pass and the room is still a mess. Rosemary's mother tells her three different things:

First Mother: "Now, Rosemary, I don't like to scold you, but you should expect me to scold you when you don't do what you're supposed to. Now, young lady, get going."

Rosemary: "But Mom, I was busy."

Second Mother: "Rosemary, when you promise to do something, I count on it. Then if it isn't done, I get disappointed and upset."

Rosemary: "Oh, OK. I'll put them away. You don't have to get mad at me."

Third Mother: "Not get mad! Huh! I really get angry when you play stupid with me. Of course, I get angry when you don't do what youre supposed to."

With which of the three comments made by her mother will Rosemary feel a closer relationship with her mom? Can you identify the destructive comment, the disguised sharing comment, and the sharing yourself communication in mom's replies?

Allow time for parent discussion and analysis. Reinforce any and all efforts.

I believe we all have the basic idea. What I would like to do next is for all of us to practice giving "sharing yourself" replies to different things children do and say. I will give you a number of examples of bad parent communication, and each time I want you to say something to the child that involves sharing yourself. To begin:

1. *Child says: "I really love you, Mommy."*

   Mother says: "That's nice, John."

What would a "sharing yourself" reply to this child be?

Wait for parents to respond. Prompt parents by giving them the initial part of their response: "I feel _____," or "When you say that, I feel _____." Continue to prompt parents in a similar way for the following examples.

2. *Child is jumping up and down on the sofa while dad is resting. Father says: "Stop being a pest or you'll get a swat, young man.*

Now, what would a "sharing yourself" reaction be?

Wait for parents to respond. (Answer: "I am trying to rest. I am very tired and I don't want to play.)

3. *Mother watches her five-year-old daughter helping her three-year-old daughter.*

   Mother says: "You are a good girl when you help your sister."

What would a "sharing yourself" reaction be?

Wait for parents to respond. (Answer: "When I see you help your sister, it makes me feel good inside; it's like seeing love.")

4. *Child Billy keeps interrupting his father while his father works on repairing the lawnmower. Father says: "Billy, now stop bothering me. I am busy. Do you hear me? Get going."*

What would a "sharing yourself" reaction be?

Wait for parents to respond. (Answer: "Billy, I am very busy and it's important to me that I finish this job soon. Each time you interrupt me, I forget what I was doing and I could make a mistake and ruin the machine.")

We all seem to have the idea of how to give a "sharing yourself" response. Can any of you think of a situation or comment of a child to which we could practice giving "sharing yourself" responses?

Pause. As parents respond, list each situation and child's comment on the blackboard. Try to get 9-12 responses. (More examples are given below. Select from these to add examples to the parent's list. At least twelve examples will be needed for the following role-playing activity). When the list has been completed, divide the group into triads. Explain that the activity they will be doing now is similar to the role-playing done previously (in Lesson 6), in which the group members took turns being the "child," the "parent," and the "observer." In this exercise, however, they will, as "parents," be practicing the use of "sharing statements," in addition to "listening for feelings" statements.

Directions for Triad Members

We are going to use the suggestions we have listed on the board to practice "sharing" statements and "listening for feeling statements." There are 12 examples, so each of you will have the opportunity to be the "child," the "parent," and the "observer." There are some specific things to pay attention to as you do the role-play.

1. The child will begin by explaining the situation and then initiate the conversation by saying his line. During the role-play he should pay attention to his feelings and reactions to the parent's responses.
2. The parent should respond by giving a "sharing" statement. Continue the conversation for 2-3 minutes using a "sharing" statement at least once more, and "listening for feelings" statements when they seem appropriate. Pay attention to your feelings during the role-play.
3. The "observer" needs to pay close attention to the "parent's" statements and to how the child seems to be responding to them. Afterwards the observer should be prepared to tell the parent how appropriate their "sharing" and "listening for feelings" statements were, and to give suggestions as to other times such statements could have been used.

After the role-play episode has been finished, take a few minutes to discuss what happened, and to get feedback from the observer.

Extra examples. (To be used in addition to parental suggestions). These should be printed on cards to be handed out to each group.

1. Sally, age, 8, has just come home from school. She runs into the living room where her mother is resting. Sally says: "Mama, please fix me some cookies and milk so I can have a picnic with June. I need them right away!"
2. Jerry, age 5, continues to run through the house after repeated attempts by his mother to stop him. Finally, Jerry knocks against a table and his mother's favorite plant falls to the floor and is ruined. Jerry, looking scared, says to his mother, "I didn't mean to break your flower, Mommy."
3. Seven-year-old Sarah makes a pretty card for her father for his birthday. She proudly puts it beside his place at the breakfast table and eagerly waits for him to read it. She says: "Happy Birthday, Daddy! I made you a card!"
4. John, age 3½, gets very frustrated while trying to ride his tricycle backwards in a straight line. After several attempts he begins to cry and scream loudly. This becomes very annoying to his mother who is trying to read nearby. John hollers, "I can't make it go right! This is a dumb tricycle."
5. Stephen, age 10, asks to help his father wash and wax the family car: "Dad, can I help you wash the car today? Then it'll look just like new!"
6. Mary, age 4, has lost her doll. This time, however, mother is visiting with a friend. Mary comes to her mother, crying, and says, "Mommy, my baby got lost again. Please find her."
7. Tommy, age 11, is responsible for taking the trash out after dinner every night. However, for the past two nights he has gone out to play softball right after dinner and hasn't emptied the trash. This is the third night, the garbage is piled up, and Tommy says: "We're getting to be good at hitting grounders, since we've practiced so much!"
8. Peggy, age 15, is busy with many activities, and is constantly asking her parents to drive her places. After making several requests during the week, Peggy comes to her father on Saturday and says, "Dad, can you take me over to Karen's? I'll call you when I'm ready to come home. Okay?"
9. Scott, age 2½, gets very mad at his mother as she tries to dress him. He hits her and says "No, Scott will do it!"
10. Laurie, age 7, has been chosen by her teacher to have the lead part in the class play. Laurie excitedly tells her parents: "Mrs. Smith is going to let me be Goldilocks in our play. She said that's a real important part!"

Before we have our break, I want to remind you that the "sharing yourself" responses help build a closer relationship with your child. However, you will not always be able to give "sharing yourself" responses, and you should not expect that of yourself or anyone else. "Sharing yourself" responses must occur from time to time if you are to have a close relationship with your child, but they will not always be possible.

Pause.

Remember, "sharing yourself" responses are not given to a child to manipulate him, to make him feel guilty, or to control his behavior. It is true that people with close relationships will consider the feelings of others and often may not do something because of how it might affect the other person. This will happen in your relationship with your child as it grows stronger. If you use "sharing yourself" responses only to manipulate and control your child, he will learn your game, and this will damage your relationship.

GENERAL DISCUSSION   Encourage the parents to discuss their personal reactions to the idea of "sharing yourself" and the application of the method to their family situation.

Now, in our next session we will practice each of the ways we have learned to help build relationships with our children. These are: 1) showing love and acceptance, 2) using reflective listening, and 3) sharing yourself by communicating your own thoughts and feelings. Therefore, I would like each of you to be sure to bring your home practice for this week to the workshop next week.

BUILDING YOUR RELATIONSHIP WITH YOUR CHILD:
PART IV—REVIEW AND PRACTICE OF METHODS

Sequence
1. Review and sharing of home practice (20-30 minutes)
2. Practicing the skills (50-60 minutes)

REVIEW AND SHARING OF HOME PRACTICE   Encourage sharing but be careful in correcting any parental errors since parents are particularly vulnerable during this sharing exercise. It would be wise to use praise and the ideas presented in Session 2 in addition to the tutoring techniques suggested in Module 22.

PRACTICING THE SKILLS   In this session we are going to use the situations that you have brought with you to practice building better relationships with your children. I would like to take a moment and review those ways.

One way is to communicate love and acceptance. This can range from simply saying you love or appreciate your child to demonstrating love by actions like touching and sharing in your child's activities — but without taking over. Two other specific ways to communicate love and acceptance are letting a child enjoy his activity without your interfering or directing and allowing a child to experience that you are a good listener.

Another way is to use listening for feelings. When you use listen for feelings, a child experiences you as understanding and accepting his feelings as well as his words. He knows you recognize his feelings. This kind of an experience increases the bonds of your parent-child relationship.

And finally, another way is to share yourself by communicating your own thoughts and feelings. The identifying characteristics of these sharing self-communications are that they usually have an "I" in them and they do not send solutions or use judgmental words.

Write three headings on blackboard as follows:
1. Communicating love and acceptance.
2. Learning to recognize your child's feelings — listening for feelings.
3. Sharing yourself.

Allow time for any pertinent discussion. Use the techniques yourself in responding to the group.

I think now we could try some of the examples you've brought this evening. Let's have a go with them.

The remainder of the time should be spent on practice. You will need to elicit how each of the three major skills could be used for virtually every situation presented by the parents. The use of role playing initially in the large group and eventually in small groups of four each is most helpful in practicing the skills. At first, you should be a major actor in the large group role playing, and later when the small groups are formed, act as a consultant and coach.

DISCIPLINE

Objectives

1. To show why extremely premissive or restrictive discipline is to be avoided, and to demonstrate that moderate discipline, whether it be permissive or authoritarian, is the most valuable.
2. To help parents recognize the extreme ranges of discipline.
3. To help parents recognize that discipline must be constructive, not revengeful. It should provide the child with a learning situation for the development of standards set by the parents.
4. To show how parental warmth moderates the effects of discipline.
5. To point out the importance of predictability in discipline. Predictability leads to emotional security and smoother functioning families.

Materials

1. Blackboard
2. Chalk
3. Eraser

References

1. Baumrind, D. Child care practices anteceding three patterns of pre-school behavior. *Genetic Psychology Monographs,* 1967, *75,* 43-88.
2. Becker, Welsey C. Consequences of different kinds of parental discipline. In M.L. Hoffman and L.W. Hoffman (Eds.), *Review of Child Development Research.* New York: Russell Sage Foundation, 1964.
3. Ginott, Haim G. *Between Parent And Child.* New York: The Hearst Corp., 1969, Chapter 5.
4. Hoffman, M.L. Parental discipline and the child's consideration for others. *Child Development,* 1963, *34,* 573-588.
5. Sears, R.R., Maccoby, E.E., and Levin, H. *Patterns of Child Rearing.* Evaston, Illinois: Pow and Peterson, 1957.

Sequence

1. Lecture-discussion (30 minutes)
2. General discussion (20-30 minutes)

LECTURE-DISCUSSION   Today we are going to discuss discipline.

Write on Board: Discipline.

For many people the word "discipline" has a harsh, old-fashioned meaning, for it has often been associated with punishment, fear, and pain. This is a negative view of discipline. However, we shall see that discipline can be basically positive and constructive. It can be a valuable method of training and guiding your child in his development by providing him with a learning situation.

OPTIONAL EXERCISE   Before we begin our discussion of discipline, I thought it might be helpful if we all tried to get in touch with our memories of how our parents disciplined us.

Long pause.

Q. Would anyone be willing to share with us some of the methods and ways their parents disciplined them. It would be best if we could think about methods that they used frequently.

Pause for parental reactions.

Q. Have these examples reminded anyone else of some of the methods their parents used?

Pause.

Q. As parents we often wonder if our way of disciplining our child is the best method. We often ask ourselves: "Am I too permissive?"

Write on board: Too permissive.

Q. Do we give our children a free rein to do whatever they want whenever they want to do it? Or, at the opposite extreme, we might ask: "Am I too restrictive?"

Write on board: Too restrictive.

Q. Do we demand strict obedience to our commands, not allowing our children to question our rules?

It is foolish to believe that if you leave a child alone and give him complete freedom, he will develop into a normal, well-adjusted adult. Overly permissive parents have gone too far in the direction of lenience. They place few restrictions on the child, allowing him to interrupt conversation at will, establish his own eating habits independent of the family, and leave his belongings all over the house. In short, overly permissive parents allow undesirable behavior from their children to develop and be practiced. When these behaviors occur outside of the house, they lead to terrible results for the child. The following is an example of an overly permissive mother:

> **Mother: "Jane, is really beginning to be difficult to put to bed at night. I tell her at 8:00 that it's bedtime, but she stays up and plays anyway. Sometimes I think she's gone to her bedroom, but then I hear her playing with her toys. Soon, she'll come out and watch TV with me and her dad. I just let her...but I would like her to go to bed when I tell her to. Oh well, if she's not in bed, she'll fall asleep after a bit anyway, and I don't want her to think I am a dictator."**

This four-year-old stays up until 10:30 to 11:00 each night, which leaves the parents almost no time to be alone with each other. The mother is too lenient. The child is getting her way at the expense of the parent's needs. This mother does not place any control over the child. In short, the child is being taught to be selfish. We know that children who have few if any controls and limits placed on them experience some problems as they grow up. The limits found in bedtime, mealtime, including rituals and traditions such as starting meals at the same time, being put to bed with a story, having your day end at a certain time, and cleaning up your toys are all very important. They help the child develop a sense of time, a feeling of security from a dependable world, and they help the child learn that he lives in a social world and he must be concerned with the feelings and rights of others.

Research shows us that the child whose parents have been overly permissive often grow up lacking in self-control. He often turns out to be selfish, unmanageable, uncooperative, and inconsiderate of his parents, friends, and spouse.

On the other hand, overly restrictive parents may think they are being strict for the sake of their child, but this strictness hides their love. Constant directions, insisting on perfection as the goal, and frequent punishment are some signs of overly restrictive parents. The following is an example of an overly restrictive mother and her son:

Mother: "It's 8:00, Johnny, and time to go to bed."
Johnny: "Oh, mom, do I have to? Why can't I stay up just a few minutes more?"

> **Mother:** "When it's 8:00, it's bedtime. Don't ask questions. Just go to the bathroom and then to bed."
>
> **Johnny:** "But..."
>
> **Mother:** "No questions...just mind mommy and do what she says or you'll get a whipping."

The child gets up slowly and mother smacks him for taking his time. This mother is overly controlling. She gives a command and expects it to be acted on immediately. No explanation is given to Johnny concerning why he can't stay up longer, except that he will get a "whipping." The consequences of this type of discipline fall into two different groups. First, either the child will learn to be timid, shy, and withdrawn from people or will develop in a self-centered aggressive way.

Research shows us that when parents are very strict, one of two things is likely to happen. First, the child develops a tendency to withdraw socially. This is an unhappy child who plays by himself and is afraid to make friends and play with other children. Second, the child of parents who are overly strict is often uncooperative, argumentative, and aggressive. It is often true that the delinquent child has been spanked more often as a young child then the nondelinquent.

With the extreme use of either permissive or severe disciplining practices, the child is more prone to develop emotional problems and anti-social behaviors like deliquency.

Finding the middle ground appears to be a key to helping your child become a mature and responsible adult.

Write on board: Moderate discipline.

Let's assume that we would like to be moderate in our discipline. The question then becomes how do we know we are not being too severe or too permissive?

Q. What guidelines can you think of that might indicate that a parent's discipline is too severe?

Pause for parent responses.

Yes, (in summary) we can see that discipline that is too severe is most often found when one or more of the following things happen:

1. The parent is very angry and not in control of his or her emotions.
2. Physical punishment is used everyday to manage the child's behavior.
3. Physical punishment or isolation is used without any warning or explanation of the effect of the child's behavior on others.
4. The parent has not carefully explained what is expected of the child.

Q. Now, what signs do you think would tell us that a parent is being too permissive?

Pause for parent response.

Well, let's summarize what you said. A parent is too permissive if one or more of the following things happens more than once a day:

1. The child is allowed to step on the rights of others while his parents are present, e.g., take toys from other children, stand on furniture in a house he is visiting, yell and scream and interrupt another adult talking to the parent.
2. The child is allowed to strike his parent or use foul language.
3. The child ignores most minor requests made by the parent without consequences.
4. The child's eating and sleeping habits are under total self-direction.

Let's consider some examples of overly permissive and severe discipline.

Jimmy's (age four) mother is having company visit at 7 p.m. Jimmy has been put in his room, but as usual, he refuses to stay. Mother and father say nothing and allow him to stay up, hoping he soon will get tired. As company arrives, Jimmy runs to the door and begins "charming" each guest. At 10 p.m. Jimmy is taking sips out of peoples' drinks, interrupting the conversation with his tumbling act, and climbing on the men's backs to play "horsey." By 10:30 Jimmy is crying and insists that mother stay in his room until he falls asleep, which is usually 11:00 p.m.

Here we see an overly permissive mother. She has allowed the child to stay up past his bedtime, jump on the furniture, and disturb her guests. If Jimmy had learned to experience and accept some limits in the past, this situation would have been different. If in the past she had explained to Jimmy why he had to go to bed, and if any problem then arose, had insisted that he remain in his room, the disruption of the party and the harrassment of the guests would have been avoided. The tragedy of this example is that children are always learning. The night of his parents' party, Jimmy learned to be self-centered, to abuse the rights of others, and to think he is the center of the world. This lesson and each one like it in the future will cause Jimmy a great deal of trouble as he tries to grow up.

Let's consider another example:

Mrs. Johnson takes her daughter Sharon, age four, to the park playground. As they enter she says: "Sharon, you must play in the sandbox. I will tell you when you can go to the swing and slide. Remember, don't get your clothes all dirty like a nasty girl." Some time later Mrs. Johnson feeds Sharon some candy piece by piece, placing it in Sharon's mouth so she won't get all messy. Sharon wanders off in the park some 100 feet to play beside a statue. Mrs. Johnson gets upset, yanks her by the hand, and gives her a swat on the rear saying: "How many times have I told you not to get out of my sight? You're just a pain in the neck."

Q. How would you rate this parent, as permissive or overly strict?

Pause. (Answer: Overly strict.)

The mother was dominating and controlling the child by giving her many commands and restrictions. In her trying to be a good and concerned mother, this woman has gone too far. She has become a dictator, a prison guard. She tries to prevent all accidents and mistakes; she demands a degree of self-control and memory that her four-year-old child, or any four-year-old child, is not likely to have. Now let's consider another example:

Mrs. Archer speaking to her son: "No, Tommy (age four), you can't have your blocks today. I know you are disappointed, but I told you you must put them away at night before bedtime. Last night I had to pick them up and I am very tired at night, and I don't want to do your work. I know your are sad, Tommy, but you will have them to play with tomorrow." Tommy cries louder. "Tommy, if you keep crying I will put you to bed. I know you are disappointed, but you can't have them." Mrs. Archer walks away.

Q. How would you rate this interaction? Is Mrs. Archer over permissive or overly restrictive or what?

Pause for parent responses.

Mrs. Archer handled her child with firmness, but it is reasonable in terms of her expectations, her consequences, and her sensitivity to the child's feelings.

Let's consider another example in which discipline is called for and let's see if we can decide on what would be moderate discipline.

Jimmy, age four, has just scribbled all over a wall in the dining room with a red crayon. This the first time this has happened.

Q. What might an overly permissive parent do? What would an overly strict parent do?

Write response on board under appropriate heading.

Q. What would moderate discipline be?

> *Answer: "Jimmy, you wrote on the dining room walls and now they are messy. I am very proud of our house and I want it to look neat. If you want to write on something big I will help you get a big paper (e.g., large shopping bag). Now you will have to clean up the mess you made. When you have cleaned the marks, you can go play again."*

Let me summarize what we have said so far:

1. Discipline is need by children.
2. Discipline should provide the child with an experience from which he can learn. This means presenting him with a clear picture of what is expected of him and why.
3. Being both too permissive and too severe causes problems.
4. All parents will be too permissive and too severe on occasion and that's OK as long as most of the discipline is moderate.

Now there is one important idea to consider about discipline and its effects on children. The destructive effects of permissiveness and overly strict discipline can be increased or decreased by the amount of love and warmth in the parent-child relationship. If the parent is very permissive and in fact has little to do with his or her child, the destructive effects of permissiveness are increased. Likewise, if a parent is very restrictive and severe in his discipline and also is distant, cold, and lacking in understanding of the child's feelings, the effects of his or her discipline will be very destructive.

How warm, gentle, and affectionate you are as a parent is important in the normal development of children, regardless of whether you are permissive or restrictive. Parents who are both warm and somewhat permissive produce children who are likely to be friendly, outgoing, independent, and self-confident. Parents who are warm and somewhat restrictive produce children who are likely to be more polite, neat, less aggressive, concerned with the rights of others, and less often in trouble at home and school. Both of these kinds of parents will raise well-adjusted and happy children.

Pause.

In short, it does not matter whether the parent uses moderate permissiveness or restrictiveness as long as he avoids the extremes and, equally important, demonstrates love and warmth. Let's consider some parent-child interactions in which warmth is involved:

> **Child:** "Dad, look at the picture I drew at school today."
> **Father:** "That's really pretty. It looks like you worked very hard and you should be pleased with your work."
> **Child:** "Yeah, it's a lot of fun too. I've started drawing a picture in the kitchen."
> **Father:** "Oh, look son, it's getting to be your bedtime."
> **Child:** "Gee, Dad, can't I stay up just a little while longer 'til I finish it?"
> **Father:** "OK, but when you're through, you'll have to go to bed."
> **Child:** "Sure, Dad. Thanks."

This is an example of a warm, permissive father. He demonstrates his warmth by showing appreciation for his son's accomplishments and praising him ("That's really pretty. You worked hard and you should be proud of your work"). We see that he may be considered permissive because he allowed his son to stay up a little past his bedtime in order to do something he considered important. Now let's consider another example:

> *Four-year-old Mary came into the kitchen while her mother was fixing dinner.*
> **Mary:** "Mommy, can I have some cookies and a glass of milk, I'm hungry."

Mother: (firm tone of voice) "No, Mary. If you eat cookies now you won't want to eat your dinner."

Mary: "Please, mommy. You don't want me to starve to death, do you?"

Mother: "Of course not, dear. But you can't have cookies now. We'll be eating dinner in 15 minutes, and I'll save these two cookies for you for a special dessert."

Q. The mother in this example can be characterized as warm and restrictive. Can anyone tell me why?

Pause. (Answer: Warm because of the friendly interchange; called daughter "dear"; gave a reasonable explanation of why she should not eat cookies now. Restrictive because she was firm with the child and did not give in to her request.)

Now let's examine some examples and see if we can figure out what kind of discipline the parent uses.

Five-year-old Tommy was watching his father mow the lawn.

Tommy: "Daddy, I want to help mow the lawn. Can I, please?"

Father: (annoyed tone of voice) "You asked me last week and what did I tell you?"

Tommy: "You said no. But can I this week?"

Father: "No."

Tommy: "Why not, Daddy?"

Father: (No response.)

Tommy: "Why, Daddy?"

Father: "Quit asking me all those dumb questions. You're in the way of the mower."

Q. How would you characterize this father and why?

Pause for parents' responses.

Q. What would a warm, restrictive parent say?

Pause for parents' responses.

(Answer: "Tommy, I would like you to help me when you get older, but a lawn mower is dangerous and I don't want you to get hurt. You cannot mow the lawn. Would you like to hold the handle with me for a while?")

This father shows warmth; he gives a reason why Tommy cannot mow the lawn (he is too young and might get hurt as lawnmowers are very dangerous; he explains why lawnmowers are dangerous and tells him when he is older he can mow the lawn.)

So far we see that:

1. Discipline is not necessarily a harsh, old-fashioned method of punishing children. Rather, it can be constructive in providing the child a learning situation for the development of the standards of behavior expected of him by the parents.
2. Permissive or restrictiveness in the extreme can have a damaging effect on the child's development. With the extreme use of either, the child is more prone to develop emotional problems and behavioral disorders.
3. Moderate discipline, whether in the direction of permissiveness or restrictiveness, appears to be the better practice and, when combined with warmth and affection for the child, provides for optimal results.

One last important point about discipline must be mentioned and that is the consistency with which discipline is applied.

Write on board: Consistency of discipline.

Inconsistent discipline occurs and will always occur. Parents are not machines. However, consistent discipline by parents in teaching their child makes the child's world more predictable. If the child knows what his mother is going to do under certain circumstances, he will know what is expected of him and how he is expected to respond. Children who are exposed to very inconsistent discipline, where the rules are always changing or are not clearly stated, have no way of knowing what will happen as a result of what they do. These children often become very anxious, fearful, or self-centered as they grow up.

It is not important that the parent do the same thing every time, since that is impossible. What he must do, however, is teach the child to predict the changing rules by pointing out the signals in the situation. For example, Dad may put the children to bed and talk with them most nights. However, on nights when he isn't feeling well or doesn't have the time, he can change the limits with "Tonight I am tired, I don't want to talk and I want you to go to bed quickly." Or mother, who normally tolerates a noisy home, may say: "I am upset about something today and I want your help. Please play as quietly as you can." By matching a particular look on your face with these words, the parent can provide another signal to the child.

Many parents find it helpful to develop a signal to their children that tells the child that the parent has had it. The child knows he is at the limit and must walk softly. The signal can be a look, some word, or both. This signal must not be overused, but must be followed through in terms of any restriction or punishment. Let me give you an example of one such signal.

> *When Mr. Jones sees Mike approach a limit, Mr. Jones will say something like the following, with the first part always being the same (in a soft and deliberate manner): "Michael, (pause), do you hear me? (pause.) I want you to sit down and watch TV or go to bed."*
>
> *Calling Mike "Michael" and using the question "Do you hear me?" is the signal to Mike. Whenever his father talks to him like that, he knows that whatever his father says next is a firm rule.*

GENERAL DISCUSSION

Q. Do any of you use a signal like Mr. Jones? Did any of your parents use a signal like that with you?

Let parents discuss this issue.

Q. Are there any questions or reactions to what we have discussed?

10

MANAGING CHILDREN'S BEHAVIOR:
PART I—WHO OWNS THE PROBLEM? AND SOLVING CONFLICTS

INTRODUCTION

MANAGING CHILDREN'S BEHAVIOR Managing Children's Behavior is a six lesson sequence which is designed to teach basic concepts of behavioral psychology. It is essential that the trainer approach this subject matter with a high degree of interpersonal sensitivity as opposed to a mechanical style. There must be no dichotomy presented between a behavioral and the more humanistic approach presented earlier. Each and every skill learned by the parents in the earlier phases of the program are essential to and compatible with the behavior principles to be taught in the following lessons. Parents must be encouraged to use their Reflective Listening and Sharing Yourself Skills while employing behavioral principles. In the context of a good relationship the behavioral principles taught will facilitate the clarification of communications and will provide structure for conflict, resolution, and for the attainment of positive goals. The ideas of using behavioral principles for imposing your will on another or of training children like Pavlov's dogs is a complete contradiction of the purposes and goals of the Parenting Skills program.

LESSON (1)

"WHO OWNS THE PROBLEM/SOLVING CONFLICTS" The trainer's objectives for this lesson are for the parents to develop an awareness that not all of their child's problems are the parents' problems and that children have a *right* to work on their own problems.

The three part framework of (1) Parent Problems, (2) Child Problems, and (3) Shared Problems is designed to help the parents analyze problems so that they are not under the continuous self imposed burden of always being responsible for the solution of all problems involving their children. Parental guilt about not helping when a child has a problem is an issue which must be dealt with. The most important counter balancing point usually is the fact that when a child works out a problem on his own, he builds strength for the future by enhancing his sense of competence. When parents come to see this point their uneasiness is usually lessened. During the discussion of shared problems the trainer must help the parents see how reflective listening and sharing yourself can help resolve conflicts or at least clarify the conflict or underlying problems.

The two exercises at the end of this lesson are designed to help the parents see the limits of the usefulness of "reflective listening" and "sharing yourself." The trainer will find that some parent dyads or triads will report triumphantly: "we tried but we are still in conflict." This awareness of irreconcilable differences is the spring board for the presentation of the idea of the need for a negotiated comprise agreement. In the event that a parent must enforce his decision or solution on a younger child the parent should be advised to recognize by reflective listening the child's feelings and not expect happy compliance. With older children, parents should be encouraged to persevere in the negotiations, since imposed solutions rarely work with teenagers.

LESSON (2)

USING BEHAVIOR MODIFICATION PRINCIPLES The second lesson in the sequence begins the process of teaching a large number of basic skills and understandings essential to the use of

68

behavioral principles in managing children's behavior. This lesson can be taught by use of either a film or a lecture discussion model. The film presentation is most suitable to parents of very young children or parents of handicapped children.

One problem which trainers frequently encounter during this phase of the training is that parents want to tackle entire problems and the process of teaching a set of skills step by step while they are concerned with a whole problem can cause some difficulty. It has been found that during the lecture discussion section it is best to keep the focus narrow and on the ideas presented in the lesson. However in the discussion following the lesson whole problems and whole solutions can be discussed. The trainer should incorporate the principles and skills of the lesson and of future lessons into these discussions. The trainer should not worry about the discussion stealing the thunder from the subsequent lesson. Parents can tolerate redundancy better than they can the ignoring of their immediate concerns.

LESSON (3)

CONSEQUENCES   In the third lesson of this phase of the training, the parents are to focus on consequences which increase and decrease specific behaviors. In discussing the concept of reinforcers, parents must come to see how this concept helps them understand the uniqueness of their child. Their identification and recognition of those things which are important to their child must be seen as a relationship building process. In fact, through good "reflective listening", the parent can most readily learn what is reinforcing to his child. Parents need to see that "sharing yourself communications," particularly those involving positive feelings are very powerful social reinforcers to children.

The skill of pinpointing specific behaviors must be presented by the trainer as an essential ingredient in parent-child communication and in developing a program of intervention. If parents appear to be having difficulty with using descriptive language it is essential that the trainer go over a number of examples ideally using the concerns of the parents in the group. It is important that the process show how misconceptions and misunderstandings occur with nondescriptive language.

LESSON (4)-(6)

RECORDING BEHAVIOR AND SETTING THE CONSEQUENCES USING BEHAVIOR MODIFICATION PRINCIPLES
The recording of behavior represents one aspect of formal behavioral contracting to which parents most often object. Further it is that aspect of programs which they most often fail to do. It is essential that the trainer communicate that the recording of behavior in a formal behavioral program must be done accurately and consistently since it can become a source of considerable anger and frustration on the part of the child. The child rightly expects an accurate and fair accounting. Problems associated with recording are some of the principle reasons why parents should be told not to use a formal behavioral program unless there exists a special problem behavior which is of great importance to them or the child. Without this special importance the motivation to sustain the program and the necessary recording will not be present. During the discussion of how to set up a behavioral program the parents must be impressed with the idea that each program must have a goal which determines when the program will come to an end. Failure to discuss this with the child at the time a program is set up can lead to negative feelings since the child loses control of when the program will end.

The trainer must be prepared to handle parent objections, biases and criticisms of behavioral principles. The trainer should maintain a nondefensive accepting demeanor and should respond to challenges in a matter of fact manner and by using his "reflective listening skills." In general, the approach which is most helpful is one which uses both reflective listening and which helps the parents pinpoint and specify the basis of their beliefs. The issue of bribing children is best handled by helping the parent see the situation through the child's eyes. Parents need to present the behavioral program as a structure to help a child reach a behavioral goal which he values. By viewing the program in this way, it represents a commitment on the part of the child to work to achieve a behavioral goal. The reinforcements serve as guides in the process of learning different behaviors, and the parent is seen as the assistant who helps the child reach his goal. If a child only receives a material reinforcement for helping his mother around the house, then the candy would be the sole basis for the change of his behavior. However, in the context of a close parent-child relationship such a reinforcer is only a fleeting reminder, a symbol of the quality of the relationship, parental praise, pride, smiles, etc. will be the sustaining force. It must be clear that many parents with good relationships and many with poor relationships use material reinforcers.

Objectives

1. To develop an awareness in parents that not all of a child's problems are the parent's problems. Children have a right to work on their own problems.
2. To help parents see how *listening for feelings, sharing yourself,* and *showing acceptance* can aid children in their problem solving.

Materials

1. Blackboard
2. Chalk
3. Eraser

Sequence

1. Review and sharing of home practice (20-30 minutes)
2. Lecture-discussion (20-30 minutes)
3. General discussion (20-30 minutes)

REVIEW AND SHARING OF HOME PRACTICE   Encourage parental sharing. However, remember that this is an area in which parents often have very fixed ideas and the discussion can get to be fairly intense. You must provide balanced support to both the permissive and authoritarian point of view. Remember successful and happy people have been raised in homes with both points of view.

LECTURE-DISCUSSION   We have talked about several topics related to building relationships with children. The main purpose of each of the recent sessions was to communicate to our children that they are worthwhile and competent individuals.

There happens to be a very close relationship between a child's feelings of being competent and worthwhile and a child's way of behaving. You can test this with yourself. When you feel really good about yourself, it is just about impossible to behave in any way other than one that shows that good feeling. When a child is feeling good about himself as a worthwhile and competent person, he will tend to behave in more positive ways. This is one of the major benefits of building a good relationship with your child based on feelings of competency and being worthwhile.

Now in this session, I want to focus on how some of the skills you have learned about building better relationships can also be used to help manage a child's behavior when the child has a problem or when you as the parent have a problem.

In a parent-child relationship, like all relationships, not everything goes smoothly; there are times when problems arise. It is not always possible to be building our relationships. There are times when there are upsets and problems in the family. These are expected and normal events that every family must deal with.

The first task of being a responsible parent during times of problems and crises is to decide who owns the problem or crises. Problems can sometimes belong to only the parent, or only to the child or the problem can be shared by all or part of the family because of a conflict in what each needs from the other.

Draw on blackboard the following diagram:

Parent	***Child***	***Parent/Child***
Problems	***Problems***	***Shared Problems***

There are many times when the problem really belongs only to the child. Often as parents we make the mistake of thinking that all of our children's problems are our problems. That is just not true or reasonable. In fact, if we behave as if this were the case, we will be undercutting and to some degree be destructive to our child's sense of self-worth and his belief in his competencies.

Children have a right to their own problems and a right to work on them.

How can you tell when a problem belongs only to your child? The simplest way is to ask yourself if this problem isn't solved or if it doesn't work out, will it affect you in any substantial way? Ask yourself: "Will I lose my job, my wife, my friends; will I be ridiculed and shamed by my neighbors, etc?" To some, the idea that a child may own a problem and that the parent may not be part of it may seem strange because parents want to help and protect their children, and that is normal. But we must learn to identify who owns the problem or crisis. Let's consider a problem owned only by a parent.

Mrs. Green has moved to a new neighborhood. She has no friends, and she misses all her old neighbors. Both her husband and her children love her and know she is lonely and sad. They care about her, but they know that she owns this problem and must solve it.

Mr. Green is working a new sales territory with a new product. He has always been a top salesman, but during the past month things haven't been going well. The people in his area have different customs and ways of doing things and he is just not accepted. Mrs. Green and the children know that Mr. Green has a problem. They care about him and love him, but they know he must solve the problem.

Before we go any further let's look at some examples of problems that belong to children, some that belong to parents, and some problems that belong to both children and parents because of a conflict of interest and needs.

Children's Problems:

1. Rose is feeling rejected by her friend Mary, who is playing with the new girl on the street.
2. Billy is upset because he can't play baseball well.
3. John is unhappy when he cannot find his toys.

Parent's Problems:

1. Your child keeps walking on the furniture.
2. Your child keeps interrupting your conversation with a friend.
3. Your child leaves his toys around the house.

Shared Problems:

1. Your child wants to go swimming and you want to stay home and work in the garden.
2. You are having company over tonight and your child wants to invite two children over for a slumber party.
3. Your youngest child cannot stand to lose when the family plays a game together, so he disrupts the game for all.

Let's consider for a moment the situation in which the child owns the problem or crisis. In this situation, my best skill as a parent is to use *"reflective listening."* I certainly don't have to solve problems that aren't mine. Further, I know children can, if we allow them to, solve many of their own problems. If I communicate to a child that I understand the feelings he has when he is upset, I also then communicate that it is acceptable to have these feelings and that the problem can really be handled by the child himself. Compare this to your own experiences of complaining about your work — whether on the job or at home. Would you really want someone to step in and solve your problems and take over?

Q. If this other person did this all the time, how would you feel about your sense of worth and competence?

Pause. Parent response.

It has been my experience that the same things occur with children. A child who is upset likes and wants to be heard and understood, but he also wants to work on his own problems, e.g.: "Mother, I'd rather do it myself." The child who has his own problems solved by a protecting parent quickly becomes either resentful or passive and dependent.

Now, let's turn to those situations in the family when the child's problem is also a problem for the parent or family. My own best skill at this point is to use a very strong and direct message that communicates how I feel or what I think; this is a "sharing myself communication." The values of this approach are many. First, it quickly lets the child know how I am affected by an upset between us. Second, it lets the child have the freedom to do something about it or to do nothing about it. Third, it eliminates a blaming or shaming message to the child — and blaming or shaming can only result in some kind of resistance. Fourth, by making an open and honest expression of my feelings and concerns I include my child in resolving the upset. Sharing myself communications signal a sense of shared responsibility rather than blaming, threatening or assigning guilt to the child.

I know, and any sensible parent knows, that "reflective listening" or "sharing yourself" communications are not going to solve the full range of problems that occur in a family. The fact is they won't. But they often help particularly where a good relationship exists. In later sessions I will share with you some ways to manage children when these methods don't work. But first, let's learn to use reflective listening and sharing yourself to help solve problems. Remember these methods of solving problems are helpful only when a good relationship already exists. In learning to use these two skills when there is an upset in the family, it first requires knowing where the ownership of the problem lies. In the following, let's identify who owns the problem — parent, or child, or parent and child.

Stimulate the participation of all parents for all four examples.

1. You discover your younger son, George, in his room crying softly. Having asked if he's hurt, you learn he's not but his feelings are hurt since the boys next door won't let him play in their clubhouse. Who owns the problem?

2. You are entertaining some friends one evening, and your teenage daughter strides in and exclaims that she has never seen so many squares gathered together in one room before. Who owns the problem?

3. Six-year-old Sarah is wandering among the playground equipment during a family picnic in the community park. As she wanders here and there, you notice she never plays with anyone or with any of the outdoor equipment. Who owns the problem?

4. Eleven-year-old Anthony wants a model airplane and has gotten permission to go across town to buy it, with the understanding that he would be back in time for dinner. Well, dinner time has come and gone. It's just starting to get dark out when in walks Anthony. Who owns the problem?

You have all carefully sifted out the important part of each situation. We can see that some parts are problems for the child, other things are problems for the adult, and some parts are shared problems.

You will also notice that each of us defined the problem a little differently; that is normal since in many situations there is no one solution or interpretation of what is important or what is happening. In these cases we can see that how we interpret the situation also determines what we might do. In general, I have found that parents, in their desire to be responsible, often define more of their children's problems as belonging to them than is reasonable to assume.

Q. Can anyone think of a problem situation which would be an example of a problem which belongs to a child?

Reinforce the efforts of all the parents who speak up. Review a few situations to be sure the concept of child ownership is clear.

Q. Would anyone be willing to share a situation in which it is not clear as to who owns the problem? Just describe the situation without letting us know what you think about who may own the problem. The rest of us will try to figure out who owns the problem or who owns what part of the problem.

Pause — Allow the parent to describe the situation and ask the other parents to try and figure it out. Reinforce all parents who speak up. Repeat this activity with as many examples as seems necessary to clearly communicate ideas.

At this time, I would like to do a role play in which all of you will collectively be my parent. In each role play, I will be the child in some of the examples we have just talked about. In doing this I would like you to get a feel for the power that reflective listening and sharing yourself can have in managing a child's behavior. I only need to make one point at this time. When the ownership of the problem is yours and you let me know it clearly, I may return to you an equally clear, sharing message. If and when I do, your best skill then is to use reflective listening until you think you can again try to reach me with your sharing of self messages. In other words, keep weighing my responses to determine whether the problem is yours or mine.

At this point role play two of the above situations. In every instance, demonstrate as dramatically as possible, and yet always be realistic, the impact that these skills have on children's behavior. Following each role play, elicit the group's impressions and summarize for them what you hear being said as well as what is being ignored.

If we are going to use reflective listening and sharing yourself as problem-solving methods, we all will need some practice. I would like you each to organize yourself into groups of four. Husband and wife are not to work together. Remember, as the parent you must decide who owns the problem and what response would be most helpful. You may need to repeat the scene two or three times until you are satisfied with your response. Group members should practice assuming each role.

Allow a few minutes for the groups' members to organize and spread out as much as possible.

I am going to give you two situations: For the first situation, one member is to be the parent and the other the child, and then you are to switch roles. The situation is to start with the child speaking to the parent.

Write the children's comments on the blackboard or hand out a script to parents.

SITUATION 1.   You are trying to have your seven-year-old learn to take care of his room. It's Saturday morning and you have asked him to make his bed and clean his room. He says: "Why do I have to make my bed and clean my room? My friends don't have to do it. You're mean."

SITAUTION 2.   You walk into the living room and find your child crying. He says: "I must be dumb; nobody likes me. I never have anyone to play with."

GENERAL DISCUSSION   OK, now I would like you all to react to how you felt about this exercise in terms of both the parent's and the child's role.

Q. Can you see how reflective learning and sharing yourself might help?

Wait for parental response.

Q. Can anyone see some problems with these ways of responding?

Wait for parental responses and attempt to help parents see the limits of these methods.

RECOMMENDED PARENTAL REACTIONS TO PROBLEM OWNERSHIP

Child Owns Problem

1. Allow child time and space to solve problem.
2. Use "reflective listening" as your first level interaction.
3. Parent may assist in problem resolution if assistance is requested by the child and the request doesn't create a problem for the parent.

Parent/Child: Share Problem

1. Parent describes problem using "sharing yourself communication."
2. Parent "reflectively listens" to child's responses and asks: "How can we solve this problem?"
3. The parent may need to repeat the first two steps before a solution is generated.
4. Comments such as: "We really need to find a solution," "There must be a way to solve this," "Let's try harder to figure this out" tend to help resolve matters.
5. The above method should not be used when the parent is unwilling to compromise or change their position. In those situations the parent should state their position and use "reflective listening." The use of parental authority in such a manner should be rare.

Parent Owns Problem

1. Parent may use "sharing yourself communications" if the child can legitimately help.
2. The parent requests assistance from the child with the understanding that if the request creates a problem for the child, the request may be ignored.

Q. Does anyone have any reactions which they would like to share about this weeks lesson?

In the coming weeks we will discuss a method of managing children's behavior called behavior modification. Behavior modification is a very powerful set of techniques for helping your child. However, like all power medicines, there are some real dangers. The most dangerous part of the methods we will consider is that the method works so well that you may get all tangled up with the method and forget that you must always be working on the quality of your relationship with your child. Your skills in "reflective listening" and "sharing yourself" must always be a part of managing your child's behavior.

11

MANAGING CHILDREN'S BEHAVIOR:
PART II—USING BEHAVIOR MODIFICATION PRINCIPLES

Objectives

1. To help parents understand that they are teachers of their children and that how they behave influences what the child learns.
2. To help parents understand that the consequences of an act determine behavior.
3. To help parents understand that it is best to change behavior in small steps.
4. To demonstrate to parents the potency of behavior modification and discuss the basic ideas of reinforcement.

Materials

1. Blackboard
2. Chalk
3. Film: **Research and Reinforcements in Learning.**
   Available from: Behavior Modification Productions
   P.O. Box 3207
   Scottsdale, Arizona 85257
4. Film projector
5. Screen

Sequence

1. Review and sharing of home practice (20-30 minutes)
2. Lecture-discussion (20-30 minutes)
3. Film (35 minutes)

References

1. Becker, W. **Parents are Teachers.** Champaign, Illinois: Research Press, 1971.
2. McIntire, R.W. **For Love of Children.** Delmar, California: CRM Communications, 1970.
3. Madsen,C.K., and Madsen, C.H., Jr. **Parents/Children/Discipline.** Boston: Allyn and Bacon, 1972.
4. Patterson, G.R., and Gullion, M.E. **Living with Children.** Champaign, Illinois: Research Press, 1968.

REVIEW AND SHARING OF HOME PRACTICE

Q. Before beginning today's lesson would someone be willing to share the results of their home practice assignment with us?

> **Pause for response.**

Q. Did anyone have any specific reactions to, or problems with, the assignment?

> **Encourage all parents to share their home practice assignment, but be careful not to pressure them. Sharing must be a voluntary act.**

LECTURE-DISCUSSION   During the next several sessions we are going to talk about and practice a very powerful method of managing children. The method is called **behavior modification.** Later in this session we are going to see a film that shows how this method

75

has been applied to change the behavior of different children in different situations. Before seeing the film, however, I would like to discuss a couple of ideas that form the basis for the method of behavior modification.

Three ideas are basic to the successful use of this method of managing children's behavior. I'll write the three ideas on the board.

> *Write sentences on board:*
> *Number 1 — We teach each other how to behave.*
> *Number 2 — Consequences of an act determine behavior.*
> *Number 3 — Behavior is best changed in small steps.*

DISCUSSION OF THREE BASIC IDEAS IN LEARNING

IDEA NO. 1: WE TEACH EACH OTHER HOW TO BEHAVE   Let's look at a couple of examples that show what is meant by the first idea.

You've just put your fifteen-month-old to bed, but he has decided that he does not want to be alone in his room. He cries and you go in to see what is wrong. You make sure there are no diaper pins sticking him, his crying stops, and you leave. In a minute, he begins to cry again and you go back in his room to check on him.

Can you see that he is teaching you how to behave and you are teaching him how to behave? He is teaching you that you are not to leave him alone. His behavior, particularly his crying, is teaching you to stay with him. At the same time you are teaching him that when he cries, you will come in his room. Let's consider another example.

Your baby is beginning to enjoy a variety of foods, so you decide to buy a jar of blackberry buckle. You give her a spoonful, and she spits it out and makes a terrible fuss. Slowly deliberately, you put the lid on the blackberry buckle and back it goes on the shelf.

> *Pause.*

You can see again that people teach each other how to behave. Your baby has just taught you not to buy blackberry buckle. People teach each other how to behave, and the closeness of the parent-child relationship makes parents and children very important teachers of each other.

IDEA NO. 2: CONSEQUENCES OF AN ACT DETERMINE BEHAVIOR   Now let's look at the second idea: Consequences are what happens after or as a result of what we do.

Suppose your son or daughter asks you: "Why does a boat float?" You feel a little funny about not knowing exactly what to say, so you just look the other way or pretend to be really interested in what you're reading in the newspaper. A little while later, your child asks: "Where does Uncle Charlie live?" Again his question is ignored. What will happen to your child's question-asking if this is your common reaction? The chances are he will stop asking questions. The consequence of his asking questions is that he is ignored. He doesn't like to be ignored, so he will probably stop asking questions. Let's look at another example.

It's Saturday morning and you are doing your grocery shopping. Your daughter asks for a piece of candy, and you tell her that she will have to wait until you get out of the store. When she hears this, she screams and throws herself on the floor and has a temper tantrum. You feel the only way to make her stop is to give her the candy, so you give her a piece and tell her to be quiet.

OK, the child's behavior in this example is screaming and throwing herself on the floor.

> *Write on board: Screams, throws self on floor.*

Q. Now, what was the consequence of this behavior? What happened after it?

> *Entertain responses and write them on board. (Answer: Mother gave child candy.)*

Right. Now the basic idea we are discussing is that the consequences of an act determine behavior.

Q. What do you think will happen to the child's tantrum behavior as a result of this consequence? Is there likely to be more tantrum behavior in the future, or is there likely to be less?

Pause for response. (Answer: Tantrum behavior is likely to increase.)

Consequences determine behavior. When the consequences of some behavior are pleasurable, then in the future there will be more of that behavior. When the consequences of a behavior are unpleasant, there will be less of that behavior. The consequences of the child's question-asking in our earlier example was that the child was ignored. This is unpleasant. In the future there will be less question-asking. In the latter example, the consequence of throwing a temper tantrum was to get a piece of candy. This is pleasant. In the future there will be more screaming and throwing herself on the floor.

IDEA NO. 3: BEHAVIOR IS BEST CHANGED IN SMALL STEPS   The last basic idea to be learned about using behavior principles is that often behavior is best changed in small steps that work toward a goal established by the parent. Consider teaching your five-year-old to make his bed. If we have him watch us make the bed a few times and them tell him to do it, what do you think would happen? Yes, he probably would get discouraged and the bed would be all messed up. He just couldn't do it.

Q. Can anyone think of a better way to teach the child to make his bed?

Pause. Wait for responses and then summarize responses with the following:

We see that there are many good ways of teaching a child to make his bed, but it is important to break the job into parts and slowly add each part as the child learns. Just putting the pillow on the bed might be the first step or just tucking in the sheet. Slowly, over a couple of weeks all the parts of making the bed would be added.

In the next several weeks, you will become more and more successful in managing your children's behavior by becoming more skilled in arranging the consequences of your children's behavior.

FILM   Tonight, we are going to see a film that shows some of the ways behavior modification has been used to help children learn. As you view the film, I would like you to keep in mind the three basic ideas we talked about so far this evening. The three ideas are again: (1) we teach each other, (2) behavior is determined by its consequences, and (3) it is often best to teach in small steps. I would also like you to notice how powerful the technique of behavior modification can be. The changes in behavior you will see are quite dramatic.

MANAGING CHILDREN'S BEHAVIOR:
PART IIa—BEHAVIOR MODIFICATION PRINCIPLES

(Alternate for Part II)

Sequence

1. Review and sharing of home practice (20-30 minutes)
2. Lecture-discussion (20-30 minutes)

How we react to our children will determine in part what behaviors they will develop, what behaviors they will continue to show, and what behaviors will disapppear. It is true that we are always reacting to one another in one way or another, so our children are always learning from us and we from them. Further, parents cannot be expected to always think of how their behavior and reactions will affect their children. In many instances, the parent's reactions are of little importance because they have to do with relatively minor and unimportant actions of their children. However, when a parent is concerned about developing, maintaining or stopping a behavior, he must begin to pay attention to his reactions to that behavior and to the situations in which that behavior might occur. This discussion brings us to two important ideas. Consequences determine behavior and children learn best in small steps.

During the next several sessions we are going to talk about and practice a very powerful method of managing children. The method is called **behavior modification.** Three ideas are basic to the successful use of this method of managing children's behavior. I'll write the three ideas on the board.

Write on board:

Number 1 — We teach each other how to behave.
Number 2 — Consequences of an act determine behavior.
Number 3 — Behavior is best changed in small steps.

IDEA NO. 1: WE TEACH EACH OTHER HOW TO BEHAVE   Let's look at a couple of examples that show what is meant by the first idea.

You've just put your fifteen-month-old to bed, but he has decided that he does not want to be alone in his room. He cries and you go in to see what is wrong. You make sure there are no diaper pins sticking him, his crying stops, and you leave. In a minute, he begins to cry again and you go back in his room to check on him.

Can you see that he is teaching you how to behave and you are teaching him how to behave? He is teaching you that you are not to leave him alone. His behavior, particularly his crying, is teaching you to stay with him. At the same time you are teaching him that when he cries, you will come in his room. Let's consider another example.

Your baby is beginning to enjoy a variety of foods, so you decide to buy a jar of blackberry buckle. You give her a spoonful, and she spits it out and makes a terrible fuss. Slowly diliberately, you put the lid on the blackberry buckle and back it goes on the shelf.

Pause.

You can see again that people teach each other how to behave. Your baby has just taught you not to buy blackberry buckle. People teach each other how to behave, and the closeness of the parent-child relationship makes parents and children very important teachers of each other.

IDEA NO. 2: CONSEQUENCES OF AN ACT DETERMINE BEHAVIOR   Now let's look at the second idea: Consequences are what happens after or as a result of what we do.

Suppose your son or daughter asks you: "Why does a boat float?" You feel a little funny about not knowing exactly what to say, so you just look the other way or pretend to be really interested in what you're reading in the newspaper. A little while later, your child asks: "Where does Uncle Charlie live?" Again his question is ignored. What will happen to your child's question-asking if this is your common reaction? The chances are he will stop asking questions. The consequence of his asking questions is that he is ignored. He doesn't like to be ignored, so he will probably stop asking questions. Let's look at another example.

It's Saturday morning and you are doing your grocery shopping. Your daughter asks for a piece of candy, and you tell her that she will have to wait until you get out of the store. When she hears this, she screams and throws herself on the floor and has a temper tantrum. You feel the only way to make her stop is to give her the candy, so you give her a piece and tell her to be quiet.

OK, the child's behavior in this example is screaming and throwing herself on the floor.

Write on board: Screams, throws self on floor.

Q. Now, what was the consequence of this behavior? What happened after it?

Entertain responses and write them on board. (Answer: Mother gave child candy.)

Right. Now the basic idea we are discussing is that the consequences of an act determine behavior.

Q. What do you think will happen to the child's tantrum behavior as a result of this consequence? Is there likely to be more tantrum behavior in the future, or is there likely to be less?

Pause for response. (Answer: Tantrum behavior is likely to increase.)

Consequences determine behavior. When the consequences of some behavior are pleasurable, then in the future there will be more of that behavior. When the consequences of a behavior are unpleasant, there will be less of that behavior. The consequences of the child's question-asking in our earlier example was that the child was ignored. This is unpleasant. In the future there will be less question-asking. In the latter example, the consequence of throwing a temper tantrum was to get a piece of candy. This is pleasant. In the future there will be more screaming and throwing herself on the floor.

Let's look at another example. Jimmy, age six, is always a slowpoke; he holds up his mother or father or the whole family when they plan to go on a trip, be it to go fishing, run errands, or visit friends. The reasons are always good ones and are always different: He can't find his shoes; he isn't dressed; he's working on something; or he can't be found. Each time, Jimmy's parents wait for him or either they or some other member of the family help Jimmy get ready. One day Jim's father decided that when it was time to leave, Jimmy would be told once, like everyone else, and if he wasn't ready, he would stay home if someone was available to watch him, or he would say in the car for fifteen minutes after they arrived at wherever they were going.

Let's look at this example carefully. The child's behavior is being a slowpoke and holding up the family.

Write on blackboard: Slowpoke, holds up family.

Q. Now what was the consequence of Jimmy's behavior for him before his father decided to change things?

Summarize. (Answer: Positive consequences, others made it easier for Jimmy.)

Q. What would you expect to happen to Jimmy's behavior given these consequences?

Parental response. (Answer: Yes, it will continue to occur or will occur more often.)

Q. Under the new procedure followed by Jimmy's parents, what was the consequence of Jimmy's old slowpoke behavior?

Parental response. (Answer: Yes, he missed many trips and family outings. He was punished.)

Q. Now what would you expect to happen to Jimmy's behavior given these new consequences?

Parental response. (Answer: Yes, he probably would work to avoid these unpleasant, punishing consequences.)

From the examples we just looked at, we can see that there are three kinds of consequences for behavior. Behavior can: (1) be ignored, which causes it to occur less often; (2) lead to positive consequences, which will cause it to continue or increase; and finally, (3) lead to negative consequences, which will cause it to be decreased or changed.

Write on blackboard: Three kinds of consequences which determine behavior —

1. Ignoring — decreases frequency of behavior
2. Positive consequences — increases or maintains behavior
3. Negative consequences — decreases or stops behavior

Let's look at some examples of situations and see if we can determine what the consequences are for the child in terms of his parent's behavior and what effects we should expect in terms of the child's behavior.

Mary Jane, age seven, is the oldest sister in a family of three girls. The youngest is age twelve months, and the next girl, age four, has a heart condition. Mary's mother finds herself very busy since she feels she must be very careful of her sick child, and she does have the baby to care for. Mary is a big help to Mrs. James and her mother praises her for helping with the other children, in fact, mother brags about it to Daddy and the neighbors. Recently, Mrs. James has become annoyed by Mary's complaints about feeling sick. Mrs. James explains to her husband how important the children's health is to her. If she sends Mary to bed, takes her temperature, feels her sore spots, and carefully listens to her complaints, which are often long and involved, it would take a lot of her time. Mrs. James feels like she is in a bind since she doesn't want to ignore Mary if she is really sick, yet she feels Mary's complaints are unnecessary.

I admit that this is a brief story and many details are left out, but can we identify the consequences of two of Mary's behaviors.

Q. First, what happens as a result of Mary's helping her mother?

Answer: Mother praises — Positive consequence.

Q. What should happen to Mary's helping behavior?

Parental response. (Answer: It should be increased or be maintained.)

Q. Next, what happens as a result of Mary's complaint about being sick?

Parental response. (Answer: Positive consequence — Mother pays attention to her alone, nurtures her, helps her feel loved.)

Q. What should happen to Mary's complaints about being sick?

Parental response. (Answer: Complaints should continue or increase.)

You will note that since we identified the consequence of what made Mary complain about being sick and we know what she wants and needs, we can readily make what she needs a consequence of some constructive behavior. In this way Mary can readily give up her crying since she will have a more constructive way of getting what she needs.

Mr. Arthur loves to make model airplanes and cars and was delighted when his son Fred, age eight, showed an interest in model airplane building. Let's look in a typical situation when Fred brings one of his models to show his father:

Tommy: "Look Daddy, I finished the model."

Father: "Well, let me see: It looks pretty good."

Tommy: "I made the wings like you said."

Father: "No you didn't Fred; you see they don't fit together properly. You just rushed through it in your usual sloppy way. (Pause.) Didn't I tell you to glue it one part at a time and wait until the first part was dried. That's why the body is crooked too. If you aren't patient, it will turn out to be a mess every time. (Pause.) It's just the same way you keep your room."

Q. Now what was the consequence of Fred building the model airplane and showing it to his father?

(Summarize parental responses. (Answer: he probably won't do it as often, or he will stop making them.)

Q. What other consequences could have decreased the chances of Fred working on model airplanes?

Summarize parental response. (Answer: Yes, other punishing consequences would decrease the chances of Fred's working on a model plane, but so would ignoring.)

Ignoring can be complete, such as looking at Fred's work and walking away, or it could be making a brief response such as "That's nice" and going on to talk about something else. The effect of such ignoring is to reduce either Fred's coming to his father or his working on model planes.

IDEA NO. 3: BEHAVIOR IS BEST CHANGED IN SMALL STEPS   The third important idea I would like to present, since it is basic to using behavior modification principles, is that behavior is best changed in small steps. One of the most common errors made by people trying to change the behavior of another person is that the teacher or parent tries to reach their goal for the child in steps that are too big. Positive consequences are achieved by the child only for a perfect or total performance since this is the only time the child is rewarded. The helpful teacher, therapist, and parent must break down the behavior to be learned or unlearned into a series of small steps with positive consequences following each step.

Let's consider the problem of teaching your six-year-old to make his bed.

Q. If we have him watch us make the bed a few times and then tell him to do it, what do you think will happen?

Pause for parent responses.

Yes, he probably would get discouraged and the bed would be all messed up. He just couldn't do it.

Q. Can anyone think of better way to teach the child to make his bed?

Wait for parent response. Reinforce all parents, and then summarize responses with the material below.

We can see that there are many good ways of teaching a child to make his bed, but in every case it is done best if the job is broken down into small steps with the child learning to do the job one step at a time.

In the next several weeks, we will all work on learning how to become successful in managing our children's behavior by becoming more skillful in arranging consequences and breaking tasks down into learnable parts.

> *Long pause. (Expressed in a slow and inviting manner): Does anyone have any reaction to tonight's discussion that they are willing to share with the rest of the class?*

12

MANAGING CHILDREN'S BEHAVIOR:
PART III—CONSEQUENCES THAT INCREASE AND DECREASE BEHAVIOR
AND SELECTING BEHAVIORS TO CHANGE

Objectives

1. To help parents understand and be able to utilize the law of learning that states that behaviors that are reinforced will increase and behaviors that are punished will decrease.
2. To help parents gain skill in identifying possible reinforcers.
3. To help parents understand that one form of punishment is withholding reinforcers.
4. To help parents identify behaviors that can be changed through behavior modification.
5. To help parents understand the importance of recording behavioral frequencies and to use this as the second step in a behavior modification program.

Materials

1. Blackboard
2. Chalk
3. Eraser
4. Workbook: "Behavior Modification Program" and "Behavior Modification Program: Sample A"

Sequence

1. Review and sharing of home practice (20-30 minutes)
2. Lecture-discussion (40 minutes)
   a. The law of learning
   b. Identifying possible reinforcers
   c. The use of punishment
   d. The importance of identifying specific behaviors
   e. Recording frequencies
3. General discussion (20-30 minutes)

REVIEW AND SHARING OF HOME PRACTICE

LECTURE-DISCUSSION   During our last session we talked about how people teach each other how to behave, how consequences determine behavior, and how it is often helpful to teach in small steps. These are three ideas that form the basis for the technique of behavior modification. As we saw in the film last week, behavior modification is a very powerful technique for teaching children. Knowing how to use this technique will make you more effective teachers of your children.

   Pause.

Let's be more specific about how consequences (reinforcements and punishments) determine behavior. As teachers of your children, you must know how people learn. The first law of learning is that behavior that is reinforced will be repeated; behavior that is punished will not be repeated. To say this another way: behaviors that are reinforced will occur more often in the future and behaviors that are punished will occur less often.

What does it mean for a behavior to be reinforced or punished? Reinforcement and punishment are two kinds of consequences. They are two kinds of things that can happen after your child behaves in a certain way; they are the result of some behavior.

For example, suppose you are working on an assembly line in a factory and you come up with an idea you feel will make everyone who is working in the plant enjoy their work more and at the same time will increase production. You take your idea to the boss and he says: "Great idea. I'd like to think about it a little longer, but I think we'll do that. You know I think your idea might win that suggestion award money." From the person who receives it, a reinforcement is something pleasant or enjoyable and a punishment is something unpleasant or something you would like to avoid. In this example was the boss's reaction to your bringing an idea to him a reinforcement or a punishment?

Pause for response.

Right, it was a reinforcement. Now, since behavior that is reinforced occurs more often in the future, the chances are that the next time you have an idea that you think is a good one, you will tell the boss about it. Now assume something else had happened when you explained your idea to the boss. Suppose your boss said: "Look, just take care of your own job. Leave the thinking to somebody who gets paid for it." No doubt you would find the reaction to your sharing your idea an unpleasant one. The boss's statement could be called a punishment, and the chances are that in the future you would not share your ideas with your boss. Let's consider another example:

Suppose on Saturday morning, completely on his own, your eleven-year-old son mows the lawn without being asked. You tell him how happy it makes you to see him do such a good job on the yard and without being asked. Would your statement have been a reinforcer or punisher?

Pause for response. (Answer: Reinforcer.)

Chances are that it is very pleasant for him to receive your praise. Since behaviors that are reinforced occur more often in the future, you have increased the chances that he will be helpful without being asked in the future.

In being teachers of your children, then, what you will want to do is to make reinforcement the consequence for behaviors you would like to see more often from your child. Behavior you do not wish to see more of, you will either not reinforce or you will punish. You might say, "Easier said than done," and you would be exactly right. In order to make it a bit easier to do, let's look more closely at what is meant by reinforcement and punishment. We said that a reinforcement or a reinforcer is something pleasant or enjoyable. What are some of the things that would be reinforcers for children?

Encourage responses and write responses by parents on board in three columns. Divide columns into categories: (1) social, (2) non-social, and (3) activity. This division is not made explicit during the volunteering of responses but will be made explicit later in the session. Be sure to get examples that fit all three categories. If these are not elicited voluntarily, stimulate examples in the deficient area by providing some of your own ideas. Some ideas should come from last week's film.

As you have given me examples of reinforcers, I have been dividing them roughly into three kinds. We might call all the reinforcers in this column social reinforcers.

Write "social reinforcers" on board above column of social reinforcers.

This column contains what might be called activity reinforcers.

Write "activity reinforcers" on board above column of activity reinforcers.

This column contains what might be called object reinforcers.

Write "object reinforcers" on board above column of object reinforcers.

All of these kinds of reinforcers are used as consequences for behavior you would like to see more of in your children. The purpose of dividing them into these categories is simply to make it easier for us to talk about the different types of reinforcers and to help you realize that there are at least three general types of reinforcers. Earlier it was said that consequences determine behavior and that behavior that is followed by reinforcement will occur more often in the future. Part of the job of the parent in teaching his child is to see that reinforcing consequences occur after behaviors the parent values. When this is done, the child learns the behavior we want him to learn.

Q. From the list we have here (point to board), what reinforcer might you choose as a consequence of your child's dressing himself for the first time if this was a behavior you would like for him to repeat in the future?

Entertain responses. Emphasize the idea that many different reinforcements are possible; each parent chooses the type he believes his child prefers or that fits the situation best.

Suppose you would like your six-year-old daughter to help her little brother more frequently. One day your little boy holds up his empty glass and your daughter says: "Would you like more milk? I will get it for you."

Q. How might you reinforce her helping behavior after she got the milk for her brother?

Entertain responses. Many are acceptable.

Very good. Again, many kinds of reinforcers would be helpful in increasing the frequency of helping behavior. Children don't need to be given M&M's or money or objects as reinforcers. In families with close relationships, social reinforcers such as kind words, words of appreciation, and praise are most often used as reinforcers. Activity reinforcers — being able to do something — can be very reinforcing. Sometimes even the closest of families will use nonsocial reinforcers such as candy and small gifts.

The other side of the coin, of course, is punishment. We have talked about punishment in previous sessions. If used wisely, when punishment is made a consequence of some behavior, it will cause the behavior to occur less often in the future. Remember, though, that punishment sometimes has an unwanted effect. Sometimes the parent's use of punishment causes a breakdown in the parent-child relationship. Frequent use of punishment can strain the positive feelings a child has for his parent. Generally, the most effective type of punishment which is least harmful to the parent-child relationship is the withholding of reinforcers. We will discuss the use of punishment in behavior modification further in later sessions when we talk about some examples of effective behavior modification programs in which parents successfully changed their child's behavior.

Pause.

Before we leave this discussion of reinforcers and punishment, there is one last important point that must be emphasized, and that is whether a thing is a reinforcer or a punishment depends on how the child sees it and not what the parent thinks. In my work with elementary schools, I often find a child whose punishment was being made to stand in the hall. The teacher reports that his behavior has not changed or has become progressively worse. That his behavior did not change may be caused by the fact that to that particular child, standing in the hall is interesting and fun. Remember the first law of learning: a reinforcement increases how often a behavior will occur. What this teacher thought was a punishment actually was a reinforcement, and that made the child misbehave more often so he could get the reinforcement. The opposite sometimes happens with what parents think are rewards.

By reinforcing behaviors that you like in your children and by not reinforcing or punishing behaviors that you do not like, you can be an extremely important influence on your child. In many ways, you can influence the type of person he is and will become. You might think of this use of reinforcement as informal behavior modification. Simply catching a child being good and reinforcing him is a powerful teaching technique.

Sometimes parents have a particular behavior that they are concerned about in their children. This may be something which you would like to see your child do more frequently, but which presently you do not see very often. An example might be helping around the house or playing nicely with a brother or sister. Or, the something which you are concerned about may be some behavior that you do not like and see too frequently in your child. An example might be fighting with other children or messing in his pants. Behavior modification is a very effective method of increasing or decreasing the number of times your child manifests a particular behavior.

There are four steps to successful use of a formal behavior modification program. The first step is to pinpoint a specific behavior.

Write on board: 1. Pinpoint specific behavior.

Let's look at one of the examples of behavior that I just mentioned. Suppose you have two sons, one age six and one age four. The two boys never seem to be able to play together for more than two minutes without getting into a fight or crying about something. You want your sons to be able to play nicely together. In order to use behavior modification to increase this kind of behavior, you have to be more specific about what it is that you want to increase. At first, you might think playing nicely together is specific enough, but it is not. The reason it is not is that playing "nicely together" can mean many different things. It can mean not hitting your brother, not crying, sharing toys, playing with your brother, or just playing in the same room and not arguing about what to play; or it can mean that little brother always lets the bigger one decide what they will do. In order to be successful in changing some behavior you are concerned about, it is necessary for you to be very specific about what you want changed. Let's go back to the example of playing nicely together.

Q. How could the parent describe "playing nicely" in a way that would pinpoint a specific behavior?

Entertain responses. Use the group to consensually validate suggestions by other group members. Ask if the response that the group member has volunteered means the same thing to other group members. Also, introduce the idea that specifying behavior includes specifying the situation. For example, "not hitting little brother when they are playing in their room" is specific and manageable.

In order to successfully use behavior modification, it is necessary to pinpoint a specific behavior. Let's look at another example. Suppose you are the psychologist and a parent comes to you and says: "My daughter is aggressive. She doesn't get along with anyone and she is always misbehaving."

Q. What specific behaviors have been described?

(Answer: None.)

Right, none. Now suppose another parent comes to you and says: "My son is shy and withdrawn. When someone he doesn't know says hello to him, he looks down at the ground and doesn't reply."

Q. What specific behaviors have been described here?

(Answer: Puts head down and doesn't respond to greeting from strangers.)

Q. What about shy and withdrawn? Are they specific behaviors?

(Answer: No.)

OK, I think you've got the idea. A specific behavior is something you can see and something which if you describe to another person there will be no doubt about what you are referring to. Here are some more examples. You tell me if they are specific behaviors or not:

1. Saying thank you when given a piece of candy.

(Answer: Yes.)

2. Getting along with little brother.

(Answer: No.)

3. Straightening up her room.

(Answer: No.)

Q. How could we make this last example a specific behavior?

Entertain responses. (Answers: hanging up clothes, making bed, putting toys away, etc.)

Q. If you wanted your child to be more independent, what specific behaviors might you try to reinforce?

Entertain responses.

The second step in behavior modification is to pick a specific behavior that you can count the number of times it occurs. How often it occurs is called its frequency. To complete the second step in using a behavior modification procedure, you must record how often the specific behavior occurs, and in what setting it occurs.

Write on board: 2. Record frequency.

Let me give you an example. Amanda's parents were concerned because Amanda was not stopping at home after school before she went to her friend's house to play. Naturally, they became worried because they could not be sure that her trip home was safe. They were concerned about a specific behavior: Amanda's not coming home immediately after school. They could count how often this happened. If Amanda did this every day without fail, they could say it happened one time per day on every school day. Sometimes, Amanda would come straight home, and sometimes she wouldn't. How often it happened might be described as a number of times per week she failed to come home. One week she may not have come twice; another week it may have been four times per week.

The frequency of a behavior tells us how often that behavior occurs in a given period of time. The frequency is a useful measure for a number of reasons. First, it helps us see how serious the problem really is. For example, it may seem like your children are always fighting when really they only fight two or three times a day. Or, it may seem like your child never feeds the dog without being asked when really he does feed it twice a week without coaxing. So, recording the frequency of a behavior helps you get a clearer idea of exactly how serious the problem is. Second, recording the frequency also helps you to see if there is any change in the behavior as a result of your trying to change it.

In recording the frequency of a behavior, it is important to be consistent about when the record is being made and how often the behavior is being corrected. For example, you may want to count every occurrence every day; or if the behavior that has been singled out occurs at mealtimes only, you would want to record its frequency at mealtimes every day. If you are not consistent about recording at the same time every day, then the changes you see in the frequencey of the behavior from day to day might not really indicate anything about how helpful your behavior modification program is. The record might only indicate that the behavior occurs more during one part of the day than another. In order to set up a formal behavior modification program, it is necessary to get a record of the frequency of the specific behavior you want to change. You want this record to reflect as accurately as possible the frequency of the specific behavior before you try to change it.

How you actually go about counting the number of times a specific behavior occurs depends partly on the behavior you have chosen to count. Sometimes the simplest method is just to have a piece of paper and a pencil with you and make a mark each time the pinpointed behavior occurs. Then at the end of the day, you just count up your marks and you have your record for the day. It is usually best to pick out one or two time periods during the day to do your recording. This is sometimes easier to handle than trying to keep a record throughout the entire day. One mother who was interested in getting her boys to share their toys chose to record the sharing behavior during a 40-minute period every evening just before it was time for them to get ready for bed.

Paper and pencil of course are not the only way to keep a record of behavior. One time, a coach of a Little League baseball team felt that the boys on the team played better and enjoyed the game more when they were praised and encouraged by their teammates. He wanted to increase the amount of praise and encouragement. To get an accurate record of how often these kinds of statements were being made by his boys, he kept his left pants pocket full of little pebbles. Whenever he heard a word of praise or encouragement among team members, he took one pebble out of his left pocket and put it in his right pocket. At the end of the game all he had to do was count the pebbles and he had a fairly accurate record. And his recording didn't interfere with his coaching at all.

We'll talk more about methods of recording in our next session, after you have had some practice with it. For home practice this week, I would like each of you to select one behavior of your child that you would like to see more of. Pinpoint a specific behavior and keep a record of its frequency during the week. All the necessary forms and instructions plus a completed sample may be found in your Workbook.

The Sample shows a behavior the parents wishes to see less of: leaving toys and clothes around the house. But remember that for your program, in order to help us learn the skills in this session and the next few sessions, I would like you to specify a behavior that you would like to see more frequently in your child — one you would like to increase. In the coming weeks, you will be able to use this behavior modification to change your child's behavior. It is important that during the first week you simply record the frequency of your child's behavior and do not try to change it. During the coming week, your counting will give you a good indication of how often the behavior occurred before the behavior modification program was begun. Please bring these records with you next week.

Q. Are there any questions before we break?

13

MANAGING CHILDREN'S BEHAVIOR:
PART IV—RECORDING BEHAVIOR AND SETTING THE CONSEQUENCES

Objectives

1. To help parents with behavior modification projects, specify exact behaviors and record it.
2. To describe additional methods of recording so that parents can develop a repertoire of recording procedures, including self-monitoring.
3. To help parents in setting consequences of behavior.
4. To show parents that to increase a behavior they must set a positive consequence.
5. To reinforce the idea that it is best to change behaviors in small steps.
6. To help parents practice setting up a behavior modification program.
7. To help parents evaluate the results of their program.
8. To help parents practice setting consequences in a behavior modification contract.

Materials

1. Blackboard
2. Chalk
3. Eraser
4. Workbook: "Behavior Modification Program: Sample B" — one for each parent group and one for trainer
5. Blank recording charts — one for each parent

Sequence

1. Review and sharing of home practice (20-30 minutes)
2. Lecture-discussion (40 minutes)
   a. Description of other methods of recording
   b. Discussion on setting consequences
   c. Practice in setting up the program
   d. Discussion on evaluating the results
   e. Discussion on practice in negotiating behavior modification contract
3. General discussion (20-30 minutes)

REVIEW AND SHARING OF HOME PRACTICE

LECTURE-DISCUSSION During the past week all of you have been keeping a record of a specific behavior of your child that you want to see changed. I hope you all have your records with you this evening. Remember we said last week that the first two steps in setting up a successful behavior modification program are pinpointing a specific behavior to be changed and finding out exactly how often the behavior is occurring, that is keeping a record of its frequency.

Q. What behaviors have you chosen to work on?

> *If no one volunteers, call on someone. Direct group reaction to the behaviors chosen. Discuss if they are specific enough to be reliably recorded. Ask if this is a behavior or an evaluation. Have several group members present what they have*

chosen to modify; then ask if anyone has a question about the behavior they have chosen. Have the group react and make suggestions if necessary.

There is quite a range of behaviors being studied. Let's see how the recording went. Recording frequencies is not always as easy as it sounds.

Q. Did anyone come up with any methods for counting the frequency of behavior that they especially liked? Did anyone have some problems with recording?

If no one volunteers, call on someone who has described the behavior they are counting. Lead the group reaction to approaches employed. Include in the discussion: Is the method reliable; is it easy to administer; where is recording taking place; can any improvements be suggested; will this method fit any other behaviors that group members have chosen to modify?

I would like to describe one additional type of recording system you might find useful. Sometimes it is possible to have your child keep a record of his own behavior. An example of behavior a child could easily record is brushing teeth. A chart can be placed in the bathroom to indicate the days of the month, and your child could just put a mark on the chart each time he brushes his teeth. This method is very easy for the parent, and children often enjoy keeping records of their own behavior. For example, if you were interested in having your child help with certain chores around the house, you could have him keep a can or a jar in his room. Each time he completed a chore, you could give him a marble to put in the jar. The number of marbles would provide a record of his helping around the house.

Pause.

Q. How might a child keep a record of his behavior if the behavior is taking out the garbage after the dinner or feeding the dog?

Pause for parent response.

Q. How about if the behavior is getting up in the morning without mother having to call several times?

Entertain responses.

There are many behaviors a child can keep a record of. Some of you may find this type of recording helpful for the behaviors you have chosen to modify.

Pause.

Let's complete the picture of the steps in a behavior modification program. We mentioned before that there were four steps. So far we have talked about the first two: pinpoint a specific behavior and recording the frequency of the behavior. The third step is setting the consequences.

Write on board: 3. Set the consequences.

A consequence, remember, is what happens after or as a result of some behavior. We said earlier that behavior is determined by its consequences. According to the first law of learning, behavior that is followed by a pleasant or reinforcing consequence tends to be repeated, and behavior that is not followed by pleasant consequences or is punished tends not to be repeated. Since you all are working on increasing some desirable behavior in your children, let's talk for a minute about how you can set consequences that will increase the frequency of a behavior. You will want the behavior to be followed by a reinforcer. You will want to set a pleasant consequence. Before, when we talked about reinforcers, we mentioned three general types: social, object, and activity.

Q. Could someone give an example of a social reinforcer?

> *Pause for reply.*

Q. How about some examples of object reinforcers?

> *Pause for reply.*

Q. And what are some good activity reinforcers for children?

> *Pause for reply.*

Let's look at a formal behavior modification program developed by a set of parents. Mr. and Mrs. Kotch were very upset by the fact that Paul, age five and one-half, was "very mean" to his two-and-one-half-year-old brother, Mark. Paul would hit Mark for no apparent reason, or would yell at him and call him names, or would pull toys away from him and knock him down. Mr. and Mrs. Kotch had tried to "share their feelings" with Paul about their concern for Mark's safety and their desire to have a happy home. Despite their increased attention and frankness toward Paul, his behavior didn't change.

Mr. and Mrs. Kotch decided to try a formal behavior modification program. They both decided to pinpoint a specific behavior. Mrs. Kotch chose the number of times Paul hit or pushed Mark. Mr. Kotch chose the number of times Paul said something kind or friendly to Mark.

time after supper and before bedtime, 7:00-8:00 p.m.

> *Put the following graphs on blackboard, explaining how to read them. Don't include treatment data.*

Graphs

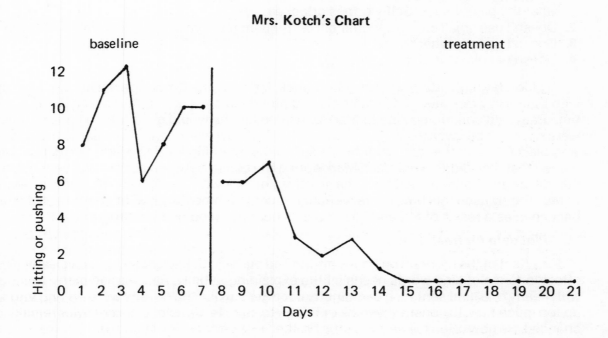

Mrs. Kotch's Chart

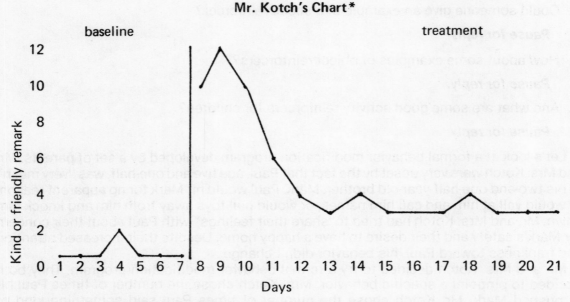

Mr. Kotch's Chart*

*Note that the job of recording was easier for Mr. Kotch.

Let's say that Mr. and Mrs. Kotch had gone about setting up the behavior modification program in another way. Let's suppose they had said: "Paul, we can't stand how you behave. You're mean and cruel. If you keep being mean, you'll grow up to be just another rotten kid. Because we love you, we are going to give you a chance to change and be nice. After supper if you are nice to Mark, you can stay up an extra 15 minutes and we will give you a snack."

Q. With the approach just described, it is not likely that Paul's behavior will change. Can you spot some of the problems with this approach?

   Parental responses. Answers:

1. Judging, scolding with your message; child is so upset he is not likely to hear the rest of what the parent·says. Self-worth is attacked.
2. Doesn't use small steps or increment or frequent reinforcements; requires "total cure."
3. Doesn't specify what to do.
4. Doesn't explain what is "mean."

The Monday night starting the second week, Mr. and Mrs. Kotch again had a conference with Paul. They repeated their concerns and proposed an agreement between them. Each time Paul said something kind to Mark or helped him he would get a roasted peanut (they were known to be favorites of Paul). To keep track of how many peanuts he earned, a marble was placed in a coffee can each time Paul said something kind to Mark. Further, it was agreed that if he didn't hit or push Mark during the period between supper and bedtime, he could stay up 15 minutes extra and have a glass of milk with Daddy while Mommy put Mark to bed. Daddy used this time to praise Paul's accomplishments. Now let me show you what happened as a result of Mr. and Mrs. Kotch's behavior modification program.

   Plot data for treatment.

The effect of the program on Paul's hitting and pushing behavior can be seen clearly. The effect in terms of kind words needs a little explaining initially. Paul earned many peanuts with nearly one kind sentence per minute, but after a while the novelty wore off and it took up too much time to constantly think of things to say. Nevertheless his behavior remained changed. He now often rewards his little brother, maybe not every minute but often enough.

You will note the Kotch's behavior modification program used all three kinds of reinforcers.

Q. What were the reinforcers?

> *(Answer: Social — Daddy's praise. Nonsocial — roasted peanuts. Activity — staying up fifteen minutes extra)*

OK, we've seen several examples of formal behavior modification programs. This time I would like all of you to set up a program. Let's divide the class in groups of three or four and work as teams.

> *Groups should be approximately equal.*

Each group will get a copy on which to outline their programs. As you will see, the first step, pinpointing a specific behavior, has already been filled. You'll have 5 minutes to decide exactly how to go about changing the behavior. Fill in the frequencies as you think they might be.

> *Pass out to one person in each group the sheet entitled:* Behavior Modification Program: Sample B. *Assist groups as needed, making sure they are very specific about recording procedures and delivering consequences.*

Q. Time is up. Let's see how you did. How did this (point to one of the groups) group go about getting Cindy to brush her teeth?

> *Group member discusses proposed program. Interrupt to get reaction from other group members as to reliability and feasibility of recording procedures, appropriateness, ease of administration of consequences, etc.*

Q. Very good. Now let's hear how this group set up their program?

> *Repeat feedback procedures.*

Some of you might be thinking at this point that behavior modification is not something new. Setting consequences is something many of you have used to manage children's behavior. For example, you might have a rule that your child can only have dessert if he has eaten his dinner, or you might have a rule that your child can watch TV only after his homework is completed. These are very definite examples of behavior modification programs and they are not new. What may be new to you is the range of behaviors that can be taught with these procedures and how to use them in a systematic way to ensure the results you are getting, particularly when the behavior to change will only change slowly because it must be learned. That brings us to our fourth and final step—evaluating the results.

> *Write on board: 4. Evaluate the results.*

Let's look at one of the examples I just mentioned — getting your child to eat his dinner. Suppose you notice that your child has not eaten any vegetables for four nights and you decide to set a consequence: he can have dessert only if he has eaten all of his vegetables. The first night he doesn't eat anything and asks you for dessert. You tell him you would like to give him dessert but the rule is he can only have dessert if he eats his vegetables. He still doesn't eat anything. The next night, the same thing happens. After five days, he still is not eating meat and vegetables. You evaluate your results and find you have not been at all successful, so you take another look at the program.

Q. Can anyone suggest why the program isn't working?

> *Entertain responses.*

Good. After you set the consequence, you continue to record the frequency of the behavior and use your record to evaluate the responses. Keep in mind, though, that usually there is not an immediate change in the behavior. Usually children will try to test you and see if you really meant what you said. When they are sure that you did mean it, the behavior will begin to change. If it does not, there is something wrong with one of the four steps in the program.

One final point about setting consequences. Setting consequences is much like negotiating a contract. The object is not to force something on a child, but to develop an arrangement that will benefit both the parent and the child. The process of setting up this contract provides an excellent opportunity for using the relationship-building type of communication we talked about in earlier sessions. It is a good chance to listen to your child's feelings and accept them. As we saw in the example of Paul and Mr. and Mrs. Kotch, the parent can best communicate by using "sharing himself" communicating, not by passing judgment. In all contract negotiations, the strongest agreement comes about when both sides use reflective listening and "sharing themselves." This give and take is a necessity. When a good interpersonal relationship exists between parent and child, an agreement can be reached in which everyone can reach their goals.

All of you have been recording a behavior during this past week. Some of you are ready to set consequences. Let's practice using these relationship-building types of communication to set the consequences. If someone will volunteer to practice setting the consequence, I will play the part of the child. Who knows what reinforcers they would like to use?

> ***Group member plays part of parent negotiating with child and you role play the child. Reinforce appropriate techniques. Call for a second volunteer; then third.***

Very good. The more you practice these techniques, the more natural they become.

GENERAL DISCUSSION

Q. Does anyone have any concerns or questions about what we are doing and how it may work in your particular family situation?

> ***Encourage and reinforce frank discussion and parents' attempts to relate the ideas to their families and their particular situations.***

MANAGING CHILDREN'S BEHAVIOR

BEHAVIOR MODIFICATION PROGRAM: SAMPLE II

Name: Cindy, age 5

Date: March 10

1. Specific behavior to be changed:

— I want Cindy to brush her teeth after dinner and before going to bed. She does this now only if we nag her about it and threaten her. —

2. Record of frequency of behavior:

Time of observation _____

_____ observations per _____
       (number)   (minute/hour/day)

every _____
             (day-week)

What will be counted? _____

| Day 1 | Day 2 | Day 3 | Day 4 | Day 5 |
| Day 6 | Day 7 | Day 8 | Day 9 | Day 10 |

3. Set consequences:

Consequences will be _____

_____

14

MANAGING CHILDREN'S BEHAVIOR:
PART V—USING BEHAVIOR MODIFICATION PRINCIPLES

Objectives

1. To provide feedback and elicit reactions concerning behavior modification projects that parents are conducting.
2. To make parents aware of Grandma's Law (Premack Principle) and understand that any activity a child enjoys can be a reinforcer.
3. To demonstrate withholding reinforcement and "time out" as methods of decreasing undesirable behavior.
4. To help parents generate answers to issues raised by the use of behavior modification.

Materials

1. Large blackboard
2. Chalk
3. Workbook

Sequence

1. Review and sharing of home practice (20-30 minutes)
2. Lecture-discussion (40 minutes)
   a. Discussion of activity reinforcers (15 minutes)
   b. Discussion of methods of decreasing an undesirable behavior (10 minutes)
   c. Discussion of common objections to behavior modification procedures (15 minutes)
3. General discussion (20-30 minutes)

REVIEW AND SHARING OF HOME PRACTICE

LECTURE-DISCUSSION   We are going to start today's session by talking about the behavior modification programs you have been working on. Some of you may only be up to recording your child's behavior, while others have begun using consequences and reinforcements. First, let's look at how the recording went for the people who are at that step.

> *Pause for parents to start discussion; if nobody starts, ask who is still on recording and ask that person to describe their procedures. Be as reinforcing as possible.*

It sounds as if everyone has a good understanding of recording procedures and the different ways they can be used. Now let's look at how the programs using reinforcers and consequences are going.

> *Pause for parents to bring up projects — if no spontaneous verbalizations occur, ask the parents directly.*
> *During the discussion bring up the importance of including in the original agreement a gradual fade-out of extrinsic reinforcers.*
> *Reinforce all efforts.*
> *Reinforce the use of reflective listening and share-yourself-techniques during the initial phase of setting up the program and in identifying reinforcers.*

Explain again that if a program is not working, it is a result of a problem in designing the program (even professional psychologists have design problems.) Parents must review (1) specific behavior, (2) recording, and (3) setting consequences.

I would like to briefly review last session's discussion of reinforcers that can be used as consequences to increase some behavior that you would like to see more of from your child. We mentioned three basic groups of consequences that can be reinforcing. The social reinforcers, such as praise and affection; the activity reinforcers, like watching TV or talking with Mommy and Daddy; and the object reinforcers, such as candy, peanuts. I'd like us to take a closer look at activity reinforcers during this session. Activity reinforcers are just as powerful as any other reinforcer, but they have two other values: (1) They usually can be fit into the regular family routine. (2) In order for parents to use these reinforcers as consequences, they have to pay closer attention to what the child does and likes and must use the communication skills of "reflective listening" and "sharing yourself" to determine what activity reinforcer will work.

⋅Let's look at some examples of parents who used activity reinforcers.

Mrs. Green was having a hard time getting her daughter, Jane, age five, to brush her teeth before she went to kindergarten class each morning. Jane would do it without any argument if her mother was there, but she just wouldn't take responsibility for it. Yelling and threats didn't seem to change the situation. Mrs. Green decided to use her reflective listening skills and said:

> *Mrs. Green: "You sure don't like to brush your teeth in the morning, Jane."*
>
> *Jane: "It's dumb."*
>
> *Mrs. Green (Remaining silent)*
>
> *Jane: "It's no fun!"*
>
> *Mrs. Green: "You would do it if it was fun?"*
>
> *Jane: "Uhhuh, like when you brush your teeth with your brush (electric brush), that's fun."*

Mrs. Green, having used her reflective listening skills learned more about Jane and was able to come up with the following informal behavior modification program using an activity reinforcer.

> *Mrs Green: "Jane, I worry about you. If you don't take good care of your teeth, you could get sick. I'll tell you what. If you brush your teeth in the morning before school without me having to remind you, you can use the electric toothbrush to brush your teeth before you go to bed."*

For Jane the reward for brushing her teeth was the chance to brush her teeth. At first it doesn't seem to make sense, but when you think about it, you see that a reinforcer is something rewarding, fun, and important to the individual receiving it. By having a close relationship with our children, by using the communication skills of "reflective listening" and "sharing yourself," you will better understand and appreciate your child and what he finds reinforcing.

Let me show you another example of how a mother solved a problem by using her communication skills, and a behavior modification program involving an activity reinforcer.

Mrs. Hand belonged to a family that socialized a good deal. Every other week on Sunday afternoon, the relatives would visit. She found that the job of getting ready was too much for her and the situation would result in much hurried preparations, yelling at the children, etc. One Sunday, she told her oldest son, James, ten, to vacuum and dust the living room and dining room. Jimmy started to do it reluctantly mumbling to himself. This usually caused Mrs. Hand to yell more. This time she decided to use reflective listening and she said:

> **Mrs. Hand:** *"James, you sure are mad about having to vacuum and dust the living room and dining room."*
>
> **James:** *"Yeah."*
>
> **Mrs. Hand:** *(Waits in silence).*
>
> **James:** *"Mom, why do I have to do this job? It's not an important job like shining the brass or silverware. I like to help, but I don't like to vacuum and dust."*
>
> **Mrs. Hand:** *"James, It's important to me to have a neat house. If polishing the brass would be important to you, then whenever company comes, I will get the polish out as soon as you finish the living room and dining room."*

This agreement solved the problem of getting willing help for the Sunday clean-up. Again, we have what some people would call harder work (the activity of polishing brass or the silver) being used to reinforce some desired behavior. Let's look at another example.

Joanie and her mother had a running battle over Joanie's homework. It wasn't that she didn't do it, but she waited until late at night to start on it and then had to stay up very late to get it finished. Joanie's mother felt that Joanie needed more sleep than she was getting. When she looked closely at the problem, Joanie's mother realized that the problem was caused by her daughter watching television after dinner instead of getting right at her homework. Joanie and her mother discussed the situation and decided on a new rule. Joanie had to finish her homework each evening before she was allowed to watch TV. The change was dramatic. Joanie began her homework promptly after dinner and still had time to watch some television and get to bed at a reasonable time.

This is an example of a very effective way to use an activity reinforcer to increase some desirable behavior. In this case, the behavior that was to be increased was doing homework early in the evening and the activity reinforcer was watching television. I mentioned last week that behavior modification was not an especially new way to manage behavior. In fact, the example I just described illustrates a technique that is so old that it is sometimes called "Grandma's Law." Grandma's Law involves arranging the order of activities. It is the technique Grandma used when she said you could have a piece of her cherry pie, but you had to take your bath first. When there are two behaviors that can occur in a situation, one that a child likes very much and another thet he may not like as much or dislikes, and you feel it is important for him to do the second one, then you must arrange it so he can do the one he likes after he does the one you feel is important. That's Grandma's Law.

Q. Is this an example of Grandma's Law?

> *"I'll take you ice-skating, but I want you to pick up the toys you've left around first."*
>
> *Pause for reply.*

That's right. It is an example of Grandma's Law. The important behavior which is less likely to occur must be done first, and the desired behavior is used as a consequence.

Q. Is this an example of Grandma's Law?

> *"Okay, you can go to the movies, but as soon as you get back I want you to rake the lawn. You know you promised me yesterday that it would be finished by now."*
>
> *Pause for reply.*

Right. This is not an example of Grandma's Law. The highly desired behavior, going to the movies, is coming first. The important behavior, keeping a promise to help, is not being taught very well.

Q. Can any of you think of other examples of Grandma's Law?

> *Pause for reply.*

There is one point I mentioned earlier that I would like to emphasize about selecting activity reinforcers for children. There are some activities that almost all children enjoy and like to do. Watching television is one example. Almost all children find watching television a pleasant experience, and if this activity is used as a consequence it is a strong reinforcer. There are some activities, though, that you cannot tell without knowing the child whether or not they would be reinforcers. For example, some young children love to set the table or dry dishes. Some like to wash the family car and rake the lawn. A very desirable activity for some children is answering the phone. These are simple, normal, everyday activities in a home and many parents miss the potential these types of activities have as reinforcers. Tuning into the activities your child particularly enjoys will provide you with a list of very powerful reinforcers. It will also have a special meaning for your child. When you suggest as a consequence activities that are really special to your child, it shows him that you know what he likes and that you understand his world at least a little bit. Suppose, for example, your ten-year-old daughter particularly likes to make Jello or brownies. One day you are particularly hurried and are trying to get the house cleaned up for some guests who are coming. You say to her:

"Honey, I really do have a lot to do and I don't think I'll be able to get everything done before our guests come. I really would appreciate your help. I'll tell you what. If you make the beds and clean the hall you can make Jello or brownies for the company."

Pause.

Since this is an activity she particularly likes, your daughter will probably help you with the housework. And at the same time, you have communicated to her that you understand what she likes and doesn't like. Watching what your child enjoys doing is one way to identify the activities that will be reinforcers.

So far we've talked mainly about increasing desirable behaviors. Generally, it is more effective to concentrate on rewarding than to concentrate on punishing. Rewarding produces both a change in the specific behavior and also can increase the strength of the parent-child relationship. Sometimes, though, it is necessary to withhold rewards or to punish in order to decrease some undesirable behavior. Let's look at some examples of how parents decreased problem behaviors by using behavior modification.

Mrs. Ward's six-year-old son, Billy, frequently soiled in his pants. She kept a record for five days and found that the soiling occurred from one to three times every day. She also discovered that the consequence of his soiling in his pants was that she washed him and changed his clothes and gave him a great deal of attention. She decided to set a different a different consequence. From now on when Billy soiled himself, she would give him clean clothes only after he had washed his pants out. On the first day with the new consequence, Billy soiled himself once. He didn't soil himself again until the twenty-first day and that was the last time it happened. Mrs. Ward was very satisfied with the results of the new consequence.

In addition to showing how one mother effectively used withholding reinforcers to decrease an undesirable behavior, the example also shows that sometimes we teach our children bad habits without knowing it. All the attention Mrs. Ward had been giving her son was very pleasant to him and served to reinforce his soiling behavior.

Here is another example of an effective method of decreasing undesirable behavior by using an unpleasant consequence.

Scott, age four, and Philip, age six, were brothers, and they frequently fought with each other over toys. The arguing and hitting was upsetting to their mother, so she told the boys of her upset and recognized that they were both angry with each other. Then she told them that each time an argument began and they started hitting each other, they would both have to sit on the steps upstairs — one on the second step and the other on the next to the top step. The boys would have to sit there for five minutes. In a few days, the number of arguments and fights had dropped from ten to twelve per day to only once or twice per day.

Scott and Philip's mother used what is called a "time-out" procedure as an unpleasant consequence. When the problem behavior occurred, the boys were made to take time out (5-10 minutes) from their playing with toys. When applied consistently, the time-out procedure can be very effective in decreasing undesirable behavior. Not being able to play for short periods is a very negative experience for children. Longer periods of time, such as 30 minutes or more, are less effective. Of course the time starts when the children are quiet and if noise occurs during the "time out" the clock starts over.

Q. Can you think of any behaviors of your children that might be handled by a time-out procedure?

> ***Pause for responses. Reinforce all suggestions.***

Usually about the time when parents are learning behavior modification procedures, they begin to develop some reservations about the procedures. There are some questions that come up fairly regularly. I would like to spend the remainder of this session helping you to decide on some answers to these questions. It might be interesting to approach the questions this way. I will be the person who has the questions and I would like all of you to play the part of someone who supports behavior modification procedures and refutes the questions I present. I'll ask the questions the way someone who does not accept behavior modification might, and you answer them the way someone who supports modification would answer. Ready?

> ***Pause for questions.***

"It sounds to me like you are bribing children?" (questioning tone of voice)

> ***Summarize parent reactions and make sure the points included in each refutation listed after the comment is covered. (Answer: Bribery involves getting someone to do something wrong or bad. Pay for honest work is entirely legitimate.)***

"What gives you the right to decide for your child what he will do? It sounds like outright manipulation to me." (irate manner)

> ***(Parents respond with something like the following: Parents make many decisions for their children. This is part of the job of parents — to guide and to teach. As we saw in the soiling in the pants incident, parents control many behaviors they don't realize. The question is not whether you will control or not, since in many ways you already do, the question is will you do it wisely and with forethought.)***

"It seems to me that you are asking us to become an 'if-then' family. If you do this for me, I'll do that for you."

> ***Parent's response (Answer: Formal contracting is not a technique you will use all the time, only part of the time. We have talked about other child management techniques. As a good teacher, though, you will always want to positively reinforce desirable behaviors.)***

"The whole thing is artificial. Kids should learn how to behave without getting paid for it."

> ***(Answer: "Should" is a moralistic, irrational concept. Kids learn what they do because of the reinforcements that follow certain behaviors. What is important is that they do learn, not whether they "should" or "ought" to have learned something different.***
> ***Regarding the artificiality, as we said, many behaviors and natural reinforcers already exist in the home; it is simply a matter of better organizing them. When***

artificial reinforcers are used, they are used to get the behavior under control; then they are slowly replaced with social reinforcers such as praise and affection, and finally self-pride in accomplishment.)

"Do you expect me to record and develop a behavior modification program to teach my child everything or to correct every problem behavior?"

(Answer: Formal behavior modification programs including recording is a special technique to be used for special problems, particularly problems that haven't been solved with less systematic procedures.)

Q. I hope this discussion has helped you to formulate some of your own answers to these questions. Are there any other questions you have?

Pause for reply. If possible get group to respond to any questions.

Very good. That is all for this evening. Continue your behavior modification projects during the coming week and pay particular attention to identifying activities that your children particularly enjoy. During the next session we will review your projects, so don't forget to bring your records. I have additional blank recording charts in the box at the door for anyone who needs them.

15

MANAGING CHILDREN'S BEHAVIOR:
PART VI—USING THE METHOD ON YOURSELF

Objectives

1. To help parents conduct their behavior modification projects with their children.
2. To point out that behavior modification procedures can be applied to oneself.
3. To evaluate objections and problems with behavior modification.

Materials

1. Large blackboard
2. Chalk

Sequence

1. Review and sharing of home practice (20-30 minutes)
2. Lecture-discussion (30-40 minutes)
   a. Review examples of behavior modification projects.
   b. Discuss the use of behavior modification with the parent's own behaviors.
3. General discussion (20-30 minutes)

REVIEW AND SHARING OF HOME PRACTICE

LECTURE-DISCUSSION Let's start off this session by reviewing the projects you are working on.

Q. How have they been going?

> *Wait for parental comments. Reinforce the first person to speak and try to get the group to respond to any questions or comments before you react.*

Q. Have any of you found the use of different reinforcements, Grandma's Law, and some of the other behavior modification methods helpful to you in ways that don't involve a formal program?

> *Pause.*

Next I would like to describe a few behavior modification programs that were developed by parents to change their children's behaviors.

Susie, an eight-year-old girl who had often been sick as a young child, developed the habit of going in to sleep with her parents in the middle of the night. Her parents wanted this behavior stopped and developed the following behavior modification procedure. First, they recorded Susie's natural behavior and found that Susie came to their bed eight out of ten nights. Susie was told she would receive a nickel every night she stayed in her bed. During the next ten nights she came to her parent's bed only two out of ten times. During the following month, she came only once and was returned to her bed promptly. After two months on the program, Susie's parents told her she didn't need the program and it was stopped. Now, it is important to note that all during the program, Susie's parents paired large doses of praise and affection with the giving of the nickel. They spoke with pride about Susie's accomplishments; in short, they made a big deal about her growing up and not doing things like she used to do when she was little.

Q. Does anyone have a reaction to this story?

Pause. Discuss and highlight the pairing of social and nonsocial reinforcers, and discuss the problem of fading-out extrinsic reinforcers.

Mrs. White wanted her ten-year-old daughter, Carol, to stop biting her fingernails. She had tried a number of methods through the years and none of them worked. She noticed that Carol chewed her nails most often when she was reading. If Carol didn't read very much in a week or so, her nails would start to grow. The idea of having Carol stop reading was just as bad as her having bitten fingernails. Mrs. White observed Carol for a week for the first 30 minutes of Carol's 1-hour reading period before bedtime. (See graph.) She then told Carol she would subtract 1 minute of reading time for each time she put her fingers in her mouth while reading. (See graph.) During the next week, Carol was punished frequently for the first three and the last two; in fact, her behavior was worse than before the program began. Mrs. White found out that Carol's nail-biting was worse when she read mysteries. When she orginally had observed her daughter and during the two days in the middle of the third week the same punishment was used, but now Carol was to read with a golf counter in her hand and each time she bit her nails she would record it.

Graph for Carol's Nail-biting

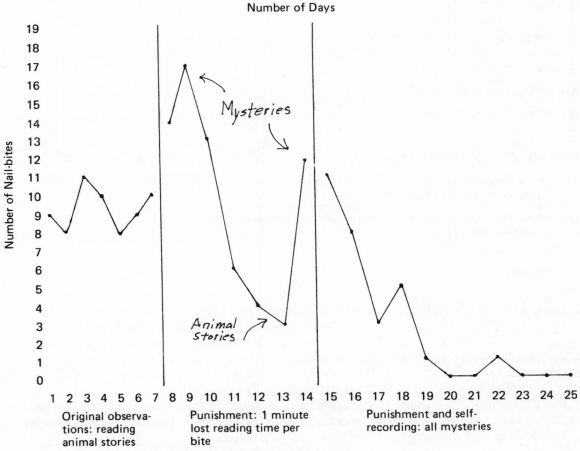

Number of Days

Q. Do you have any questions about this program?

Discuss the problem of baseline recording under similar conditions. Highlight different self-recording procedures for children, e.g., stars on charts, graphs by the bed or in the bathroom.

Mrs Patterson was unhappy with her youngest son Mark's behavior which was very dependent. Mark, age four, was frequently whining and playing under Mrs. Patterson's feet. He seemed to have frequent minor hurts, and he would not get out his own toys to play with. Mrs. Patterson found herself too often helping, holding and "making it better" for Mark. She realized she was reinforcing his behavior with her attention — the very behavior she didn't like. She decided to ignore, as much as possible, all of Mark's dependent behaviors and to reinforce his independent behaviors, such as playing by himself for ten minutes or more, fixing his own scrapes, and getting out his own toys. (See graph.)

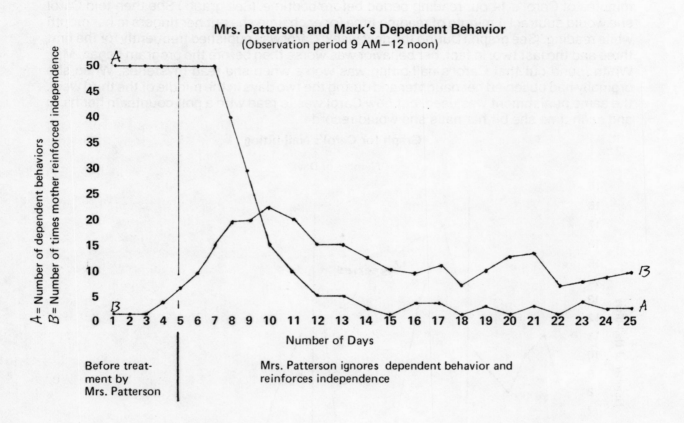

Mrs. Patterson and Mark's Dependent Behavior
(Observation period 9 AM—12 noon)

A = Number of dependent behaviors
B = Number of times mother reinforced independence

Number of Days

Before treatment by Mrs. Patterson

Mrs. Patterson ignores dependent behavior and reinforces independence

The graph shows us that Mrs. Patterson rarely reinforced the behaviors she wanted to see and that since she responded to Mark's independent behavior, she reinforced the very behaviors she disliked. The combination of ignoring dependent behavior and rewarding independent behavior worked, but not immediately. We can't always expect immediate results from our programs; in fact, in some cases as with temper tantrums, things usually get worse for three or four days, before they begin to bet better.

The other important point to be noted in the graph is that Mrs. Patterson's behavior changed. Mark was occasionally dependent as all four-olds are, but Mrs. Patterson was not a mother who was training her child toward independence.

Behavior modification programs may be looked at as ways of changing other people's behavior, but it is interesting that the programs do as much to change the behavior of the parent as they do to change the behavior of the child. Some of the changes found in the parents' behaviors after running a behavior modification program are:

1. Closer attention to the child's specific behavior and needs.
2. Greater consistency in the parent's behavior.

3. More rewarding and reinforcing behavior of parents toward their children.
4. Greater sense of self-confidence in managing children's behavior.
5. Catching children being good more often and reinforcing the behavior they want, which creates a whole new outlook on managing children's behavior.

So far we have talked about several ways behavior modification procedures can be used to change children's behavior. Before leaving the topic of behavior modification, I would like to mention one other approach.

Sometimes an effective way to manage a child's behavior is by focusing on and making changes in the person who is teaching him. For example, in one of our earlier sessions, we talked about the importance of reflecting a child's feelings — that is, responding to the feelings behind what the child says rather than to the words he uses to express his feelings. Reflecting feelings is a behavior many parents are not accustomed to and they frequently feel a little uncomfortable with doing it at first. A simple behavior modification procedure can be used to help you over this initial period and make reflection feelings a habit for you. You can keep a record of how often you reflect your child's feelings by keeping a tally, or moving some sort of counter from one pocket to another, or one of several other ways we mentioned for recording. At the end of the day, write down your score and keep a daily chart to see how well you are progressing. Often, seeing you own progress is enough of a reinforcer to keep you at it, and soon the benefits in terms of improved parent-child relationships will be a very powerful reinforcer. After a short itme, reflecting feelings will seem very natural to you.

Often parents can help one another. For example in one family in which the husband wanted to stop yelling and hollering at the children the wife agreed to wash her husband's car Sunday afternoon if he could go seven days without yelling and hollering at the children more than twenty times. Each night they would record the number of times he hollered. On succeeding weeks, a new agreement was reached — no more than fifteen times, then ten, then seven, then five, and then two.

You can also help yourself with Grandma's Law. For example, you would love to take the kids to the park on Saturday, but the game is going to be on TV. Simply tell yourself you can't watch the game until you have taken the kids to the park.

Pause.

Or, you would like to finish the ironing, but a good show is on TV. Rather than have the dessert before the vegetables, get the ironing done before the show comes on.

Q. Can you think of other behaviors you can effectively manage with the procedures we have talked about?

Entertain replies.

Last week we discussed some objections people sometimes raise about behavior modification.

Q. Now that you have had some more experience with the technique, can you think of any other problems or objections?

Pause. Write objections or problems on the blackboard; don't respond or attempt to refute the parent's comments. Merely collect the reactions and list them on the blackboard. When all of the objections have been raised, direct the group to respond.

Q. What do you think about the first problem listed? Can things be handled such that this would not occur?

Summarize parents' reactions and then complete the responses if you believe some important point was missed.

The behavior modification procedures we discussed are very effective ways of managing behavior. They are often used by psychologists and psychiatrists to treat serious behavior problems. You can use these procedures by either designing a specific program or by just keeping in mind the idea that reinforcers increase behavior and that ignoring decreases behaviors.

I would strongly recommend that in the future, you only use a specific formal program on the few behaviors that are either very disturbing to you or are of greatest importance. Behavior modification is a powerful tool, but formal programs take time and energy which may create more of a problem than the behavior that is of concern to you.

Q. Do you have any questions or reactions?

> *Pause. Respond to questions and reactions — Praise parents using "constructive praise."*

16

MANAGING YOUR FEELINGS:
PART I—PARENT-CHILD INTERACTIONS

Managing Your Feelings

Introduction

This introduction will focus on the 4 session sequence entitled **Managing Your Feelings.** The concepts presented in this sequence are based upon the principles and techniques of Rational Emotive Therapy (RET). While not all trainers will be familiar with these concepts, a number of well written books are available to the trainer from the Institute of Rational Living, 45 East 65th Street, New York, NY 10021.

The first two readings suggested below are most directly related to the use of RET principles with children while the second two readings are most helpful in developing the trainer's background in relation to parent to parent interactions.

The first lesson in this sequence entitled — Managing Your Feelings, Part I — Parent Child Interactions, is designed to teach three major understandings. First, to help parents recognize that when people are experiencing strong negative emotions their problem solving ability is usually reduced. Second, to help parents see that when interactions occur between a parent and a child that the parent is interpreting the interaction and assigning it meaning. This spontaneous and instantaneous process may be best understood as a form of self talk. Third, parents are to be guided into an appreciation of the fact that the feelings and emotions which occur in any situation are a direct and automatic reaction to the self talk. The preceding understandings must be presented and illustrated so that the parents are ready to have the trainer present the ABC model; as much time as is needed by the parents should be devoted to these initial three understandings. Following the presentation of the ABC Model, which is midway in the first lesson, it is often most helpful for the trainer to encourage parents to produce examples of situations which happen between them and their child (A), and their self talks (B), and their feelings or reactions (C). The trainer's purpose in encouraging this spontaneous production is to reinforce the fact that there is a "self talk" at point (B) regardless of how brief or fleeting the thought.

The second half of this session is best presented by having the trainer develop on the blackboard a chart similar to the Practice Sheet for ABC Analysis. As the trainer presents the remaining information in this lesson he should make extensive use of the chart. Samples of these charts are to be found at the back of the Parent Workbook. While presenting the concepts in this lesson the trainer should project the understanding that what occurs at point C is a logical and inevitable consequence of the Self Talk at point B. Emotions and reactions therefore, while related to situations which occur, are caused by the self talk at point B. By having parents work through an A-B-C Analysis in reverse they can often predict the likely self talk at point B. Another additional technique which is helpful is to have the trainer describe two situations and then have parents write down on 3 x 5 cards their emotional reactions to the situation on the front and on the back their self talk. The cards are then shuffled and redistributed to the parents. Each parent then reads the emotional reaction and guesses with the group what the likely self talk was to have produced the given emotional reaction. In this anonymous way the parents get feedback and they can discuss the various self talks which are possible. This discussion is quite helpful since it should reduce the tendency for the parents to think that because I think something about a situation it is the right or only reasonable way to view it.

MANAGING YOUR FEELINGS — PART II: PARENT-CHILD INTERACTIONS   The second session in this sequence is in many ways the most critical lesson in the sequence. It is here where the trainer most often begins to receive parental feedback which rejects or is critical of the RET approach to managing their feelings. These parental objections usually cluster around three ideas:

1. That this is just a way of rationalizing and denying problems.
2. That the parent would be a phony if he used the idea since emotions are natural and just happen.
3. The inability to give up the idea that "he made me mad" or "he made me feel guilty" as the correct way to view the world.

These objections must be accepted as natural and reasonable reactions to a new way of thinking. Parents are to be reassured that the A-B-C analysis is not to be applied to all situations but it is most useful when a given situation occurs again and again and the same negative emotions and upset occur again and again. The ABC analysis will permit the parent to see if it is not helpful and/or irrational.

MANAGING YOUR FEELINGS — PART III: PARENT-PARENT INTERACTIONS   The third lesson in this sequence often produces some of the liveliest discussions since the parents have now had an opportunity to try the ABC analysis in specific situations. Given their normal reactions to their children, parents will try to enlist the support of others for their self talks or will challenge the trainer by suggesting he just does not understand the situation. At this point, it is best if the trainer allows the parents to answer each other's questions as much as possible. Multiple sources of input and the group process tend to facilitate change and acceptance in individual parents. Another strong factor in stimulating discussion is the section of the Parent Workbook in which they examine 8 common self defeating ideas. These ideas are often recognized as the basis of some of their self talk and it is both reassuring and upsetting. We have found that often the discussion surrounding the homework engages so many of the parents that the trainer may want to postpone a scheduled lesson to allow the parents to have a session devoted to sharing their situations and reactions.

The focus of lesson 3 is the parent-parent reaction. This lesson has the potential to create conflict between spouses in the group particularly if they don't have a strong interpersonal realtionship. If the trainer can anticipate the problem it can be handled by restricting the focus of the discussion to parent-parent interactions in relation to their child.

One positive technique which has been employed when parent couples are involved in the training is to have them role play and act out situation A from their homework. The class then writes down what they think the reaction at C will be and the self talk at point B. The class then discusses the reaction and the probable self talk that each party to the interaction had. The couple who did the role play must watch and listen to the discussion but may not participate in it until some degree of group consensus has formed.

Before concluding this introduction it must be pointed out that this sequence, "Managing Your Feelings" is one which new trainers often report as being one of the most stressful portions of the program for them. On the other hand it is one portion which parents often judge to be the most helpful to them. It should be recognized that in many ways this sequence is the most challenging to the parents' self image and identity. It is recommended that if a new trainer plans a series of short courses with a group of parents that he not use short course #1 which covers this sequence first.

Objectives

1. To acquaint parents with the rational-emotive theory of behavior.
2. To demonstrate how rational-emotive theory can be used in analyzing parent-child interactions.
3. To suggest an approach for parents to use in increasing rational control over their overt and covert responses in parent-child interactions.
4. To help parents begin to investigate their self-talk in problem situations involving their children.
5. To provide parents with practice in demonstrating and encouraging the use of rational-emotive theory in their parent-child interactions.

Materials

1. Large blackboard
2. Chalk
3. One 5x8 file card for each parent
4. Workbook: Managing your feelings — Part I"

References (for units 16-19)

BASIC READING

1. Ellis, A., and Harper, R.M. *A Guide to Rational Living.* Englewood Cliffs, New Jersey: Prentice-Hall, 1971.
2. Ellis, A., Wolfe, J.L., and Mosely, S. *How to Prevent Your Child from Becoming a Neurotic Adult.* New York: Crown Publishers, 1966.

SUPPLEMENTAL READING

1. Ellis, A. *Reason and Emotions in Psychotherapy.* New York; Lyle Stuart, 1962.
2. Ellis, A., and Harper, R.M. *A Guide to Successful Marriage.* New York: Lyle Stuart, 1970.

Sequence

1. Review and sharing of home practice (20-30 minutes)
2. Lecture-discussion (40 minutes)
3. General discussion (20-30 minutes)

REVIEW AND SHARING OF HOME PRACTICE   How are your projects going? Would anyone like to share with us how their project is going? Is anyone having problems with their project or is anyone disappointed in the results? Does anyone have any specific questions about their project?

LECTURE-DISCUSSION   During this session I will present a method we can use to help us manage our feelings and behavior. Hopefully, in the next few weeks, we will all come to see that we can control our feelings and reactions and that they are for the most part not determined by what happens in a given situation. Each of us will come to learn that we own our emotions.

When people get angry they often do things they later wish they hadn't done. For example, a parent may spank a child because he is angry or upset, or a wife may not speak to her husband for an hour or more because his coming home late from work was topped off by dinner being burned. If the parent in the first example or the wife in the second were to be questioned about their behavior, they might reply something like: "I couldn't help it, I just got mad," or "He made me so damn mad, he's just lucky I didn't throw something at him."

Of course, anger isn't the only emotion that often leads to stupid behavior. Other negative emotions, including guilt, fear, depression, and anxiety also may lead to stupid behavior. Let's consider some common examples of situations that lead to strong emotions and possibly stupid behavior.

Mrs. Smith told her two boys ages four and five that she was going to wax the kitchen floor this afternoon, and she wanted the boys to be sure not to step on it until it dried. That afternoon, two minutes after she had finished the floor, the boys burst through the kitchen door and ran through the kitchen. At that moment, Mrs. Smith says to herself angrily: "How inconsiderate! (Pause.) They don't care about how much work I do, and they obviously don't care about how I feel."

Q. What do you think happens next in this story?

Put responses on blackboard.

Q. How do you think this mother will feel toward her children?

Pause for parents to react.

Right. The boys get a good scolding and probably get spanked because Mrs. Smith is angry. Given what Mrs. Smith said to herself about the situation, it is obvious why the boys were scolded and spanked. But it is possible that this incident could have turned out differently.

Pause.

Let's imagine that the boys run through the kitchen and Mrs. Smith says to herself: "I knew it! I should have locked that door. When those boys get to playing tag, it's a miracle that they don't run into a tree."

Q. Given this second example of self-talk, what do you think probably would happen?

Pause. Discuss the possibilities of Mrs. Smith getting angry and the boys getting scolded or spanked following the second example of self-talk (Probable reaction: Remember to lock door in future. Ask boys to watch her finish reparing damage before resuming play.)

The example of Mrs. Smith shows us that often there are different things we can say to ourselves about situations, and that what we say to ourselves will lead to different reactions.

Let's consider another example.

The Jones family is getting ready for lunch, and while nobody is noticing, Mary Beth, age three and one-half, tries to pour a full half-gallon of milk into her glass. The next thing that happens is a great splash! Milk is all over the place! Mother turns and thinks (expressed dramatically): "How many times have I told her not to touch the milk carton. She is a stubborn little girl and she is going to have to find out who is boss."

Q. What do you think Mother is likely to do next in the story?

Pause to get parent reaction.

Q. How will Mother feel toward Mary Beth?

Discuss probable event.

I guess from what was said it is safe to assume that basically you agree that after Mary Beth spilled the milk, her mother became angry and she probably scolded, and maybe punished, Mary Beth.

Let's replay the last example again.

Now let's say that the milk has just gone splash! Mother turns and says to herself (Exasperatedly): "Oh no! I worked so hard on the floor and just look at Mary Beth's dress. I have just got to teach that child what she can lift and how to pour."

Q. What do you think is likely to happen next?

> ***Pause. Discuss probable events.***

Now again, in the second example both sets of self-talk are possible. Both could take place, and again, each would probably lead to a different reaction.

> ***Give examples of likely consequence, e.g., mother not angry, remembers to teach her in future, requests Mary Beth to clean floor, etc.***

These examples demonstrate something that most people tend to forget; and that is that events and other people don't determine what we do and feel. Rather what we say to ourselves about situations determines our reactions and how we act. Let me draw a diagram here which we are going to use a number of times in this session and in the next few sessions. I believe this diagram will help us understand and keep in mind what determines how we act.

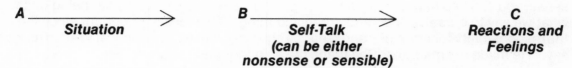

A ——————————————⟶	B ——————————————⟶	C
Situation	*Self-Talk*	*Reactions and*
	(can be either	*Feelings*
	nonsense or sensible)	

Now, one important thing to consider about the things we tell ourselves is whether or not they make sense. Are the things we say to ourselves sensible — do they agree with the facts? In most instances, would other people agree with what I am saying to myself? Let us consider some situations A and the idea of the senibility of self-talk.

SITUATION I   Mrs. Smith is having a party at her house for grown-ups. Her only child, Jimmy, age three, has been playing in his room alone for some time. He comes out of his room and says to his mother in front of her company: "I hate you. These people are just a bunch of stink bugs."

> ***Pause.***

Following this incident, Jimmy's mother gets angry, feels hurt, and punishes the child. This is the reaction C.

Q. What did she probably say to herself in her self-talk B which let to her reaction?

> ***Draw out idea of rejection — he doesn't love me, mother is embarrassed — other mothers think I am a bad mother. (Answer: I'll show you. If you hurt me, I'll hurt you.) Ask the group to decide if it is sensible for this mother to believe her child really doesn't love her.***

Now let's assume that Jimmy's mother doesn't get upset at point C and talks to the boy briefly in a gentle manner.

> ***Pause.***

Q. Given the second set of reactions, what did the mother say to herself at point B?

> ***(Answer: "Poor fellow, we have been ignoring him. I guess he was just desperate for attention. I guess the girls now know I have a spirited boy. Nevertheless, I am going to have to show Jimmy I don't like what he did, and show him the correct way to get my attention.")***

In the first reaction Jimmy's mother's self-talk was not sensible and it led to her punishing him. In the second reaction, her self-talk was sensible and it helped her find a way to teach the boy what she expected of him.

Now let's consider another situation.

SITUATION II   Mr. Jones spots his son Johnny, age three, sticking hair pins into the electric outlets. He rushes over to him, pulls his hands away from the outlet, begins scolding the child, and spanks his hands.

In this case B probably went like this: "That's dangerous! He could get seriously hurt. I must stop him now and try to insure that he doesn't do it again. I don't like to spank and yell but what choice do I have?" Given this self-talk, his actions are understandable and, importantly, they are sensible and rational. Here the emotional upset and punitive behavior C makes sense. If Mr. Jones had said to himself: "What Johnny is doing is dangerous, but if I let him get a shock, he will learn his lesson." The likely consequences of this self-talk would be for Mr. Jones to do nothing. His self-talk would not be sensible.

The way of looking at behavior which I am presenting is not Pollyannish; I am not suggesting that every cloud has a silver lining. There are times when fear, anger, sadness, and guilt are reasonable and sensible reactions. However, this is not true if these feelings occur frequently and/or last for a long period of time. Now, if what I have said so far makes sense, you can see that it is not only things and children that lead to our being upset, but what we say to ourselves about children and things. This idea is important since it places the responsibility for emotions and feelings squarely with each individual We can no longer say: "He made me mad," or "She made me so angry that I spanked her."

Pause. Speak slowly and deliberately in explaining the next point.

Clearly the A-B-C model shows us that we have a choice. Our reactions and feelings at C are not determined completely by what happens at A. What we say to ourselves at B and how sensible it is will determine what happens at C.

Now let's consider some of the common objections raised about the A-B-C model. Some people will say if I tell myself something different from my natural reaction, I will be a phony. That's a nasty word to call oneself. I can see why a person who might say this to himself wouldn't want to try using the A-B-C model. Who would want to do something that would make himself feel like a phony?

But let's see if that sentence is sensible. To begin, we all have beliefs and ideas that guide how we act. But does anyone believe we were born with them? No! We learned them. Sometimes we were aware of trying to learn them, and other times we were not. We may have copied a favorite older cousin's way of saying things by practicing what he said and how he said it. We also learned our moral beliefs although we may not be able to recall how. Your practiced bahavior and your unconsciously *learned* moral beliefs both are equally real and not phony parts of you.

Now if you begin to think in a different way, say using the A-B-C model, it will feel strange, just like learning a new language would be strange. Would you be phony for learning a new language? No! Obviously, then, all that remains is that you feel uncomfortable. Well, it probably is worth feeling a little uncomfortable if it will help make you a more effective and sensible parent.

Pause.

Another first reaction to the A-B-C model which one sometimes hears is: "Well, with your point of view, you would excuse everything children do and place all the blame on the poor upset parent." This reaction is made up of two parts, both of which are false. First, there is nothing in the A-B-C model that says anything about excusing ineffective and unacceptable behaviors in children. Parents and families have standards and limits for children's behavior, and both are reasonable and needed for the child's sake as well as the parent's. The A-B-C model may help the parent, upset at point C, to look and see what it was in points A and B that lead to the upset. For example, a father is upset that his child leaves his toys around the floor in the playroom and doesn't put them away when he is done playing.

Pause.

Now it is reasonable to expect a five-year-old to pick up and put away his toys. If the father gets upset and spanks the child, he probably said to himself: "I have told him a thousand times and he just wouldn't listen. He is begging for it. If I don't teach him to be neat now, he probably will be a hippie-slob when he grows up."

If the parent in this case would examine the situation using the A-B-C model he would say to himself: "What am I saying in B that is causing me to be upset?"

   Pause.

What part of what he said is sensible and what part is nonsense? Let's examine some of the sensible self-talk this father might engage in.

Sensible Self-talk —

1. It is sensible that a child of age five can be expected to be responsible for his toys.
2. It is sensible and it is important that a child be responsible for his possessions.
3. It is sensible to expect a child to pick up his toys at the end of the day.

   Now let's consider some of the nonsense self-talk in the above example.

Probable Nonsense at Point B —

1. It is probably nonsense for the father to expect a five-year-old to put his toys away when he is finished playing with them during the day. How does the child know he is finished playing with them?
2. It is probably nonsense to believe that the child was "begging for it." It is not likely that a child wants to be hurt.
3. It is probably nonsense to believe that picking up toys has anything to do with being a hippie.
4. It is probably nonsense to believe that the child should want to share the parent's concern with neatness. It would be nice if a five-year-old shared his father's concern for neatness, but is it reasonable to expect a five-year-old to be concerned with neatness?

Let's consider two other examples: First, imagine a father, watching his seven-year-old son and his friend playing football on a large field near their house. This field is used by all the neighborhood boys as a football field. Suddenly a large group of older boys comes along and tells the younger ones to get lost because they have a big football game. The father watches as his son and friend walk off the field disappointedly without arguing. The father has a strange mixture of emotions: He is furious, hurt disappointed. When his wife asks why he is upset, he relates the story saying: "Margaret, our son just let himself get pushed around. He never stands up for himself. (Pause) I don't know what to do. He gets it from me. That's just the way I was when I was a boy, and you know how the guys at work treat me."

Q. Now what is A?

   Pause. Write parents' responses on board.

Q. What is C?

   Pause. Write parents' responses on board.

Q. What is B?

   Pause. Write parents' responses on board. Make sure the following points are made about the probable nonsense the father was telling himself:

1. Question whether this piece of evidence is typical of the child's behavior.
2. I feel worthless and now I will have a worthless son.
3. That a child ought to stand up for his rights at all times, and that it is terrible and awful to retreat. It makes more sense to stand up for your rights and get a beating than to retreat from an impossible situation.

That's good! I think we are all getting good at handling the examples I have given you. At this point I would like to try to experiment with the ideas we have been discussing.

Q. How many of you can remember being alone in a dark room when you were young?

Pause.

Good. This should be easy for you. I am going to turn off the lights in this room and I'd like all of you to close your eyes and try to recall being put to bed and lying in the dark.

Shut off the lights and speak softly.

I want you to try to remember those feelings, (pause) concentrate on remembering just how it was.

Pause. Wait 30-45 seconds.

Now let's see how many different feelings we had. Would you each describe the feelings you had and how you behaved when you were young.

Write on blackboard all the C parts of reactions, leaving room for A and B.

Now, I would like you to tell me what the B was that you told yourself and that led to your feelings.

Pause.

What other thing might you have said to yourself that would have caused something different to happen at C?

Write responses on blackboard.

To summarize, before we conclude, we all know that no situation or person causes us to get upset and angry. Whether we get upset or not depends on how we evaluate the situation; that is, what we say to ourselves. If we are concerned and annoyed, it may be because our self-talk is sensible. But it may be that our frequent anger and upset is caused by some nonsense we have told ourselves. It becomes our job for the future to be aware of what we tell ourselves about situations and to discover whether what we say to ourselves is sensible or nonsense.

OK! Now, I think we all have the general idea of the A-B-C model.

GENERAL DISCUSSION   Are there any questions or reactions? Did anyone have a reaction to tonight's lesson that they are willing to share? Mr. Smith, you seem to be uncertain or concerned about what was said...

INSTRUCTIONS FOR HOMEWORK   This week for homework you will have some situations to analyze in your workbook. After you complete the workbook assignments, I would like each of you to write on a card or piece of paper a description of some situations at home with your child that often lead to your being upset. Describe the situation and your upset, including the things you usually do and say. Please don't sign the card or paper or put your name on it. We will use these descriptions next session to practice the A-B-C model on each other's descriptions. We will keep the identity of the writer of each description secret.

17

MANAGING YOUR FEELINGS:
PART II—PARENT-CHILD INTERACTIONS

Objectives

1. To review rational-emotive theory of behavior.
2. To help parents in applying rational-emotive theory in parent-child interactions.

Materials

1. Meeting room and chairs for approximately 20 people
2. Large blackboard
3. Chalk
4. Box labeled "Place Cards with Problem Situations Here"

Sequence

1. Introduction and review (3 minutes)
2. Questions and reactions (9 minutes)
3. Small-group discussions of homework problems (30 minutes)
4. General discussion (20-30 minutes)

INTRODUCTION AND REVIEW

As parents arrive have them place their anonymous problem situations, which have been written on cards, in a shoebox at the door. Supply cards to any parents who forgot to bring theirs.

Good evening. I'm sure you will recall that last week we discussed the A-B-C model of emotional behavior. Since we will be referring to it several times this evening, I'll draw the diagram on the board again.

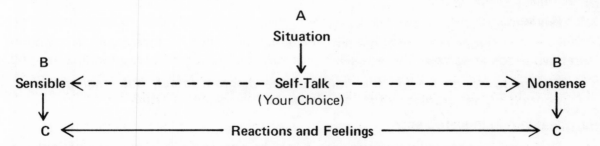

Remember the point that was made last week about behavior.

Point to C.

Our reactions are caused mainly by what we tell ourselves about the situation.

Point to B.

They are not totally caused by what happens at point A. This means that our reactions partly depend on our self-talks or how we evaluate the situation. When our self-talks are sensible, they lead to effective problem-solving. When our reactions to the same situation are repeatedly strong, negative emotions, like anger, the chances are that our self-talk has been "nonsense."

> *Pause.*

Q. Are there any questions about the A-B-C model or the material covered last week?

> *Pause. Wait until some interaction begins. Entertain questions.*

Okay, the first thing we are going to do this evening is go over the home practice problems. Let's break up into groups of four people each. Be sure you don't get in the same group as your husband or wife. I'd like each group to go over the answers to each of the four problem situations. In about 15-20 minutes, I will ask the groups to report on the answers they have come up with.

> *Small-group discussions of home practice problems.*
>
> *Go from group to group, making sure each is on task and provide assistance with the analyses. Look at anonymous problem situations turned in by parents at beginning of session.*
>
> *After 10-15 minutes, call on one group for answers to homework problem number 1, a second for the answers to the next, etc. For the fourth situation, write out the entire analysis on board in following form:*

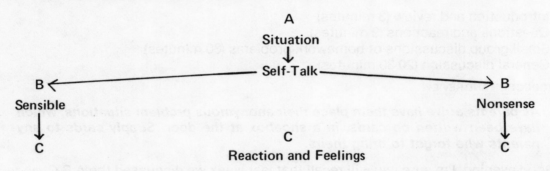

GENERAL DISCUSSION   That's very good. You've come up with some ideas that show you are thinking about the model.

> *Pause.*

Now that everyone has had some practice with this technique, let's return to our seats and have a look at some of these real-life problem situations you brought in this evening.

> *Return to board, leaving the frame of the diagram intact, but erasing the content of last problem situation. Read the first problem situation.*

Q. What ia A in this problem?

> *Wait until parents volunteer answers. It may be a struggle for them, so a patient and relaxed manner would be very helpful. Direct class through the analysis, filling in each of the spaces in the diagram as parents supply the answers. Procedure is repeated with a second problem situation and a third, and as many as time allows. Important: emphasize that situations can be evaluated in a number of ways and some of these evaluative thoughts make more sense than others. If we examine the sensibility of our evaluative thoughts, we may prevent negative emotions and promote effective problem solving.*
>
> *Note the tone of this discussion. By communicating acceptance in your words and tone of voice, you can prevent this exercise from deteriorating into*

judgments of right or wrong, good or bad. Rather, there are many different possible self-talks — some help improve matters because they are based in reality; others don't help, or make things unnecessarily worse.

Parent involvement in working out answers to the problems in this class discussion is vital to the success of the unit. Do not supply your own answers. There may be a long pause before the first volunteer offers an answer, but wait it out. Verbally reinforce parents' responses, particularly at the beginning of the discussion.

For home practice during the next week, I would like everyone to continue examining their interactions with their children and pay particular atention to the self-talk in those situations which involve anger or upset. This can best be done by sitting down after such a situation and writing as best you can remember the self-talk by which you evaluated what happened. You will find in this week's home practice some blank forms that you can use to help you analyze your situation. The home practice also contains a discussion of eight common self-defeating ideas that frequently lead to nonsense self-talk. These ideas, when examined carefully, are often found to be part of people's self-talk when strong, repeated emotional upsets occur.

18

MANAGING YOUR FEELINGS:
PART III—PARENT-PARENT INTERACTIONS

Objectives

1. To review the rational-emotive theory of behavior.
2. To demonstrate how to apply rational-emotive theory to parent-parent conflicts and personal problems.
3. To discuss some possible objections to the rational-emotive approach.
4. To provide practice in analyzing problem situations.

Materials

1. Large blackboard
2. Chalk
3. 5x8 cards, 1 for each parent

Sequence

1. Lecture-discussion (20 minutes)
2. Small-group discussion of problem situations (20-30 minutes)
3. Review and sharing of home practice (20-30 minutes)

LECTURE-DISCUSSION   Good evening. For the last couple of weeks we have been discussing the A-B-C model of emotional behavior. You will recall that emotions like anger, fear and depression are not caused by just the situation itself, but are caused by the situation plus what we tell ourselves about the situation. I will draw the diagram that we used before.

> **Draw the following diagram on board.**

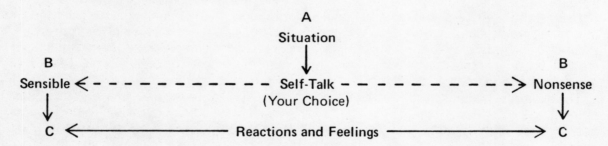

A is the situation or event, B is the self-talk which may be either sensible or nonsense, and C is the reaction and feelings. What happens at C depends on A and B.

So far we have been discussing situations and problems involving parents and children. We have found that when the parent's self-talk in a situation is sensible, the reactions and feelings that follow are also sensible. Good problem solving results from sensible self-talk. Of course parent-child problems are not the only ones that can benefit from sensible self-talk. Consider the following situation.

> **Fill in blanks in diagram on board as you read the script. See instructor's diagram at the end of this lesson for correct responses.**

Mr. and Mrs. Smith have just returned home from a party. It used to be that every time the Smiths went to a party, they would argue all the way home and for the most of the next day. But tonight there is no argument. Mrs. Smith thinks she knows what has made the difference. She has learned how to manage her feelings. When they go to parties, Mr. Smith drinks more then Mrs. Smith would like him to. In the past his wife would get quite upset about this. She recalls having self-talks that went something like this:

> *"He shouldn't drink so much, he is making a fool of himself and embarrassing me. (Pause.) How awful! What kind of a wife will my friends think I am if my husband gets drunk all the time and does not respect me. Nobody will like us."*

But tonight Mrs. Smith is not angry and she is not upset. When she examines her self-talk this evening it goes something like this:

> *"I wish John wouldn't drink as much as he does at parties. But he is responsible for his behavior. I guess he drinks to help himself unwind and he is not obnoxious when he drinks. Our friends certainly seem to like him, or they wouldn't invite us to all of their parties."*

> *Pause.*

The A and B sections of this situation have been described and have been written on the board.

Q. In the past when Mrs. Smith's self-talk was about being embarrassed and her husband being a fool, how do you think she behaved and felt?

> *Pause for response.*

Given Mrs. Smith's new, sensible self-talk, we see that she wasn't upset or ashamed of her husband for drinking more than she thought he should. This time we have no fighting and no anger.

> *Write: no anger, no fighting under sensible C.*

You can see how Mrs. Smith managed her feelings. She examined her self-talk, made sure it was sensible, and then she could behave in a more reasonable way.

During the past two weeks, we have shown how the A-B-C analysis can be used in improving parent-child relationships. With this session and the next, we will practice using the A-B-C analysis in a variety of situations, not only for those involving children. But before we look at some of these other situations, let's examine some of the objections to the A-B-C analysis that generally arise after a few weeks of practice with it.

The example that was described this evening of the Smiths at the party might have raised at least one objection. Some of you may be thinking that the A-B-C analysis forces you to accept a lot of things that you would rather not accept. It forces you to surrender. For example, when Mrs. Smith's self-talk was sensible rather than nonsense, she probably decided that it would be best if she did not nag her husband about his drinking at parties. In other words, she accepted the fact that he would drink when they were at parties, and he might drink more than she wanted him to. So she did accept something she didn't like. She lost the "drinking at parties" battle because this time she refused to make it a battle.

One of the very important lessons for an adult to learn is knowing when to fight. That is, learning to recognzie which issues or situations will be improved by fighting them and which ones will not. The A-B-C analysis helps you to decide which issues or situations deserve battles and which do not. Let's look once again at Mrs. Smith's self-talks. The nonsense self-talk was based on the idea that Mr. Smith was making a fool of himself, that Mrs. Smith's friends would consider her a failure as a wife, and that her friends would not like her anymore. When she examined these three self-talks, it seemed that Mr. Smith was not such a fool, or at least the rest of the people at the party did not think so. She also realized that the idea that his drinking indicated that she was a failure as a wife was not sensible since they continue to be invited to their friends' houses. You may recognzie that the final self-talk, the idea that her friends would not like her anymore, is one which was discussed in the Workbook from last week.

Certainly Mrs. Smith needs friends and it is important to her that she be liked. But how much is she willing to pay for this? Is she willing to battle her husband every week over the number of drinks he is allowed? It seems that in the past Mrs. Smith held the self-defeating idea that it was necessary to be constantly loved and approved by everyone. It is likely that it was this self-defeating idea that led her into battle with her husband after every party. She was afraid that someone would disapprove of her and she would do whatever she felt she had to to avoid such disapproval. The A-B-C analysis allowed her to see that the real issue, the issue that should be attacked, was her unlimited need for constant love and approval. In the past, she had been upsetting herself, not examining her self-talk, and attacking her husband for drinking too much. The battle went on every week because the real issue, the self-defeating idea that constant love and approval is necessary, could not be settled. It was not being dealt with.

It is a fact that when conflict or bad feelings exist between the parents and these occur again and again over the same issues, we know that these arguments are based on some nonsense or self-defeating idea held by one or both parents. These problem situations cannot be solved until both parents examine the sensibility of their self-talks.

So, the A-B-C analysis does not encourage surrender. It encourages us to be more selective in our fighting. By examining our self-talk, we can see what the real issues are and we can deal with then in more constructive ways.

Pause for parental reaction.

We believe that when parents apply the A-B-C analysis to those interactions between themselves which frequently lead to anger or hurt feelings, they can strengthen their relationship. It is a well known fact that the better parents interact, the more competently and reasonably they raise their children and the happier their children will be. Also one of the most powerful ways children learn to behave is by watching the behavior of the people around them, especially people they love. If you want your child to develop the ability to analyze his self-talk, you could share with him, at least once in a while, your self-talk. You could show him what the sensible self-talk would be and what the nonsense might be. In this way, he learns that he has a choice and you are teaching him to be sensible and how to control his feelings. This modeling of self-analysis assists the child by discouraging denial and repression of thoughts and feelings.

Pause for parental reactions.

We have shown how the A-B-C analysis can be applied to improve parent-child relations and parent-parent relations. It is also useful in helping us get along with ourselves and solving strictly personal problems. The following example illustrates how the A-B-C model can be applied to a personal problem and also illustrates one of the self-defeating ideas mentioned in last week's handout. The example comes from a recent television show.

A hospital was developing a new program for people who had cancer. There is a great deal of fear and dread associated with cancer. It is truly a frightening disease. It is also true, however, that people can live many years after having contracted certain forms of cancer. The aim of the new program that the hospital in the television series was developing was to help control the spread of cancer in a patient and to help the patient handle his fears concerning having cancer and dying. The approach seemed to be successful in general, but one patient was just not buying this approach. The doctors could not convince her that the remainder of her life was worth facing. She was deeply depressed and refused treatment.

Of course it doesn't make sense to refuse treatment when one is sick, and the emotions this woman was experiencing were decidedly negative. Let's analyze this situation using the A-B-C model.

Use diagram on board.

The A of course is the woman has cancer.

Write on board under A: Cancer.

The C on the nonsense side is that she is deeply depressed and is refusing treatment.

Write on board under C nonsense: Refusing treatment.

Q. What could the self-talks be that let to the nonsense C?

Write down parents' answer. Bring out the idea that the woman is not accepting reality, she is saying: "it shouldn't happen to me, if I am disfigured no one will love me."

Q. What self-talks would have been more sensible in this situation?

Leader writes parents' responses on board.

Good. And at C, here, we would probably have no depression and the woman would accept treatment. In this example, the woman's insistence that reality should not be the way had led to depression and very poor problem solving. Self-talk that contains the idea that some event or person should or ought to be different is always nonsense. We may wish at times that reality were different, but to say that it should be different suggests that there are not reasons for its being the way it is. The idea that reality should be different is not only illogical, it is self-defeating. Reality is the way it is, and saying it should be different does not lead to mature acceptance of reality or to good problem solving. It generally leads to negative emotions like depression, self-pity, and anger.

It may sound like I am saying that, as a result of attending these sessions, no one here should ever experience another negative emotion. I do not mean that at all. What I do mean is that by examining the self-talk in a situation, you can make a judgment as to whether or not your reactions and feelings are reasonable. At first, you will probably react and feel much the same way you did before attending these sessions. The only difference may be that after experiencing an emotionally charged situation, that is after A, B, and C have already occurred, you might sit down and take a closer look at what has happened. You might find that at least part of the self-talk at B was not totally sensible and that your reactions and feelings at C were not as reasonable as you would like them to be. But as we mentioned before, the kinds of situations husbands and wives get upset about usually are repeated again and again. This means you will have another chance to challenge and get rid of the nonsense portion of your self-talk. The task is a difficult one, and it may only be accomplished through practice.

Q. Are there any questions about any of the topics we have covered so far this evening?

Entertain questions.

SMALL-GROUP DISCUSSION   OK, now we are going to divide into groups of four. This time I would like husbands and wives to be in the same groups. Each group is going to receive two problem situations involving adults. The situation described can serve as A in the A-B-C analysis. I would like each group to complete the analysis, including the possible sensible and nonsense self-talk and reactions and feelings. We will then present some of these analyses for the class to discuss.

Parents break into groups. Hand out two problems to each group and assist the groups. Allow groups to discuss situations for 5-8 minutes, then direct attention

of class to the front of the room and call on one group to supply an analysis of first situation. Each of the situations provides an example of at least one of the common self-defeating ideas from last week's handout. Stress the self-defeating idea behind the nonsense self-talk. Repeat procedure for all six of the problem situations.

PROBLEM SITUATIONS FOR SMALL-GROUP DISCUSSION

1. Mr. Brill was an accountant and a very successful one. However, he was not a very successful mechanic. On weekends, he frequently got himself involved in working on the family car. Most of the time he created more problems than he solved. What self-talks could Mr. Brill choose and what might be his reactions and feelings?

2. Mrs. Buck was a housewife and not a happy one. Her life seemed meaningless and the routine she had gotten into really seemed like a rut. What self-talks could Mrs. Buck choose, and what might be her reactions and feelings?

3. Mr. Rush got off work at 4:00 P.M. and after a very hectic day he was anxious to get home and relax. He waited for the bus and when it came, he realized that he only had a $10 bill. The bus driver said: "Sorry, Mac. No way I can change $10. You'll have to get change somewhere and catch the next bus." "Don't give me that! Look, just let me ride home tonight and I will give you the fare tomorrow," said Mr. Rush. The bus driver said: "Hey Sport, I can't let anybody on the bus without paying the fare. Got a schedule to keep. So long." What self-talks could Mr. Rush choose and what might be his reactions and feelings?

4. Ralphie enjoyed his job very much. He was doing something he had wanted to do for a long time. The only part of the job he didn't like was his boss. Ralphie knew that if he performed well on his job, he could get a promotion and make more money. But he really disliked his boss. Sometimes Ralphie worked hard to get his promotion, but sometimes he did the least he could. What self-talks could be influencing the amount of work that Ralphie does and what are his feelings and reactions likely to be?

5. They had had such a beautiful relationship. At least that is what Nancy thought until Ned suddenly left her. What self-talks could Nancy choose and what might be her reactions and feelings?

6. In the past, Gladys used to get upset because George would come home from work obviously troubled about something and refuse to discuss it with her. She used to get upset and then feel very depressed. She is beginning to be successful at refusing to upset herself. She is trying to change her self-talk. What were her self-talks and reactions in the past and what are they now?

REVIEW AND SHARING OF HOME PRACTICE

Q. Would someone be willing to share their home practice exercise with the class?

The home practice for the coming week asks you to analyze two situations according to the A-B-C analysis. One of the situations or events can be in relation to anything or anyone, but one must be between you and your spouse. The more openly and honestly you do this assignment, the greater its benefit to you. Your task will be difficult since you will be challenging some of your lifelong beliefs.

At our next session we will go over any of the situations you are willing to share. There will be a box in the room to deposit your home practice sheets when you arrive next week. We will go over each set of situations, self-talks, and reactions. Please don't sign your home practice or use real names so that we can work on each situation anonymously.

INSTRUCTOR'S DIAGRAM

A

(SITUATION)
MR. SMITH DRINKS AT PARTY

SELF-TALK

B. SENSIBLE

1. I would like him to drink less.
2. He works hard.
3. Drinking helps him unwind.
4. No one else seems to mind his behavior.
5. He's not obnoxious.
6. He doesn't hurt anyone.
7. He is responsible for his own behavior.

B. NONSENSE

1. He shouldn't drink so much!
2. He is making a fool of himself.
3. He is embarrassing me!
4. How awful!
5. People will think I'm a failure.
6. People will not like me.

C.

1. Not angry.
2. Not upset.
3. Asks husband if he wants coffee.
4. No fighting.

C.

1. Made herself angry.
2. Fought with husband.
3. Didn't talk to husband.

A

WOMAN HAS CANCER

B. SENSIBLE

1. I hate having cancer.
2. What lousy luck.
3. There's not a thing I can do to prevent it.
4. I can slow down its progress and enjoy life while I have it.

B. NONSENSE

1. It shouldn't happen to me.
2. How awful, I will die.
3. No one will love me if I am disfigured.
4. Just let me die — now.

C.

1. No depression.
2. Accept treatment.

C.

1. Depression.
2. Refuse treatment.

PROBLEM SITUATIONS FOR SMALL-GROUP DISCUSSION — LEADER'S GUIDE

1. Mr. Brill

B. SENSIBLE
1. No one is good at everything.
2. Car repair is just not my "thing."
3. I'm not going to upset myself because I am not a good mechanic.

C.
1. No upset.
2. Seeks help with difficult work.

B. NONSENSE
1. This is embarrassing.
2. Men should be able to fix cars.
3. I'm not good at anything.

C.
1. Angry at himself.
2. Depressed.
3. Continues to frustrate himself.

2. Mrs. Buck

B. SENSIBLE
1. I'm bored.
2. I'm not presenting myself with enough variety or challenges.
3. I better do something about it.

C.
1. No upset.
2. Takes steps to provide herself with variety and challenges.

B. NONSENSE
1. Life is meaningless and I'm worthless.
2. Things should be different.
3. This is a terrible situation.

C.
1. Feels just awful.
2. Pities herself often.
3. Sits around feeling depressed and does less each day.

3. Mr. Rush

B. SENSIBLE
1. If he would have let me on the bus I'd be on my way home now.
2. I suppose he has no reason to break the rules, but I wish he would have.

B. NONSENSE
1. That jerk.
2. He burns me up.
3. He should not have done that.

C.

1. Not angry.

C.

1. Angry and upset.

4. Ralphie

B. SENSIBLE

1. I can't stand that guy, but I'm not going to jeopardize my chances of getting a promotion because of him.

C.

1. Works hard to get promotion.

B. NONSENSE

1. I'll show him.
2. I'm not going to wark hard for a guy like that.

C.

1. Does not work hard in attempt to get back at boss and probably does not get promotion.

5. Nancy and Ned

B. SENSIBLE

1. I really miss Ned.
2. I feel rejected.
3. I wish he hadn't left.

C.

1. Feels sad for a time, then works on new relationships.

B. NONSENSE

1. I just can't go on.
2. He left me; I must be worthless.
3. I'll be miserable, that will show how much I loved him.

C.

1. Depressed, forlorn, becomes inactive.

6. Gladys and George

B. SENSIBLE

1. I wish he could share his feelings with me. It might make him feel better.
2. The more upset I get the less likely he is going to share his feelings with me.

C.

1. Not upset.

B. NONSENSE

1. He should share his feelings with me.
2. He thinks I'm stupid and couldn't help
3. I'm a lousy wife.

C.

1. Upset, depressed.

19

MANAGING YOUR FEELINGS:
PART IV—PARENT-PARENT INTERACTIONS

Objectives

1. To provide directed practice for parents in analyzing situations in their lives that lead to negative emotions.

Materials

1. Blackboard
2. Chalk
3. Box placed at entrance to room and labeled: "Place Problem Situations Here"
4. Extra paper and pencils

Sequence

1. Introduction and leader's sample problem (10 minutes)
2. Group discussion of problem situations supplied by parents (50 minutes)

As parents arrive have them place home practice with problem situations in box at door.

Good evening. I hope everyone has remembered to bring in a problem situation. I have some paper and pencils here. We have a few minutes before we begin, so anyone who has forgotten to bring in his problem situation or would like to offer another one, please feel free to do so.

Pause two or three minutes, allow parents to fill out card.

INTRODUCTION AND LEADER'S SAMPLE PROBLEM   During the last three weeks we have been talking about how to manage your feelings by using the A-B-C model. We have shown how this method can be used in different situations. Tonight we are going to talk about the problem situations you have brought in. Before we start, I want to be sure you know that these situations will be talked about without using your names. Sometimes people feel a little uncomfortable about writing down a real-life situation about themselves or themselves and their spouse, but remember that no names will be used.

This is the final session on managing your feelings. It is important that you have the experience of listening to others use the A-B-C model for your own situations because in the weeks to come, the class will be talking about different things. The usefulness of this new technique you have learned of managing your feelings will depend on how well you can figure out problem situations by yourself or with the aid of your spouse. The session this evening should be quite helpful in providing an example for you to follow when you are on your own.

I will draw the outline on the board again.

Draw following diagram on the board.

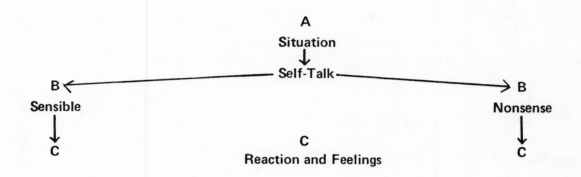

SPECIAL SESSIONS

(Suitable as Single Lectures or Presentations)

(1) developing your child's intelligence
(2) special education
(3) helping with school work
(4) special education—PL 94-142

20

DEVELOPING YOUR CHILD'S INTELLIGENCE:
THE YEARS BEFORE SCHOOL*

Objectives

1. To present the ideas that a child's intelligence is not fixed at birth and that, in part, how smart or dull a child will be depends on his early sensory and social experiences.
2. To aid in providing sensory experiences (exercises) to help your child develop his intelligence.
3. To aid in providing language experiences and physical experiences to help develop your child's intelligence.

Materials

1. Trainer should bring to the session sample educational and homemade toys.
2. One copy of "Your Child's Intellect" should be available for parents' inspection.

References

1. Bell, T.H. *Your Child's Intellect.* Salt Lake City: Olympus Publications, Co., 1972. (This is an excellently illustrated book which should be of great value to an interested parent. It provides a developmental understanding of a child's intellect, plus activities for children ages one to six.)
2. White, Burton L. *Human Infant: Experience and Psychological Development.* Englewood Cliffs, New Jersey: Prentice-Hall, 1971.

Many parents think their child's intelligence is something that is fixed at birth and cannot be changed. This is simply not true. It has been said that this is one of the most important educational discoveries of the twentieth century. It is so important that I will repeat it: A child's intelligence is not fixed at birth. A child's level of intelligence is determined in much the same way as his strength. When children eat well and exercise their muscles, they grow strong and develop fully. With proper food and proper exercise, the brain also develops fully. In this session we are going to be talking about how parents can provide the proper exercise or stimulation for their children's brains; that is, how parents can help their children develop their intelligence.

At this point someone may be thinking: "Why parents? We have too much to do in bringing up our children as it is, and now you are giving us the responsibility of making our children smarter. That's what we send kids to school for. Now I suppose I'll be asked to run a school at home." If any or all of these thoughts have crossed your mind I would like to answer them this way: Only recently have psychologists and educators begun to realize how important the years before school entrance are for the development of a child's ability to learn. It is widely believed now that most of the child's basic intelligence has been formed by the time he reaches school age. This, of course, does not mean that by the time he is six years old, he has learned most of what he will know as an adult. What it means is that most of a child's ability to learn quickly and with ease has developed by the time he reaches school age. The experiences and exercises the child receives in his early years are very

*This unit is designed for parents of children below six years of age.

important in determining how smart he will be. The people who are in the best position to supply these important experiences and exercises are the child's parents. How willing most parents are to accept responsibility for assisting their children in developing their intelligence depends on two things: First, knowing how to help their child's intelligence develop, and second, knowing how easily the activities can be built into their daily routine.

Before we discuss some of the activities and exercises we can use with our children, I would like to mention three important ideas. First, as parents, we are our children's first teachers. We help them form their attitudes toward learning and it is important to make their earliest experiences positive and pleasant ones. When learning is a pleasant experience, the child learns that discovering new things about this world is fun and he will approach new situations with enthusiasm. The second important idea is that it is important to remember that a young child has a short attention span; he is not able to concentrate on one activity for long periods of time. Sometimes he will play with his blocks for ten or twenty minutes, but other times he may want them for only a minute or two. There is no benefit in forcing a young child to do things he is not interested in doing. This only makes him feel that these activities are not fun and ought to be avoided. Whenever your child's interest in some activity fades away, stop it immediately.

A third point to consider in helping your child develop his intelligence is educational toys. There are hundreds of toys on the market and they all claim to be educational. Actually, no toy in itself is educational. It depends on what the child does with the toy. Two goals should be kept in mind when you buy toys. First, will it help the child exercise his brain and sensory systems? Examples of good toys for infants are those which exercise the senses. Good examples of such crib toys would be Fisher-Price Activity Center, and Kohner's Disney Musical Box, along with most sturdy crib mobiles. It is important that toys for three- and four-year-olds assist in developing ideas such as size, number, time, and organization. The second goal is that they should help learning be fun. You will find in your workbook sets of criteria for selecting toys for children of various ages as well as commercial toys which fit these criteria. The child should enjoy playing with his toys. Of course, some of the best educational toys are items found in every home such as pots and pans, boxes, measuring cups, pencils, and paper. Many sensory-stimulation activities may be obtained from normal household equipment used as an educational toy.

What kind of experiences and activities help to develop a child's intelligence? The answer to this question depends mainly on the child's age and existing level of development. Let's look first of all at the child in the first year of life. During the first few months sensory experiences — hearing, seeing, touching, smelling, tasting — are very important for the child. He is developing an awareness of the world around him and he comes to know his world through his senses. A young child's brain, and therefore his intelligence, is exercised when he has different experiences and gets different information from his senses. The basic senses, remember, are seeing, hearing, touching, smelling, and tasting.

Write these five senses across top of blackboard.

To these I will add moving since the child also experiences sensations involved with the movement of his body.

Add "moving" to the list on board.

Q. Who can think of some good ways to exercise a child's senses during the first few years of life?

Entertain responses from parents and briefly note these responses under appropriate senses on board. Be prepared to assist in stimulating responses. Be sure to stress activities that are enjoyable for the child and consistent with normal parental activities.

These are all good ways to exercise a child's senses and stimulate the development of intelligence.

Let's now look at some of the things that help develop the intelligence of the twelve-to-twenty-month-old child. One of the most important things is the language the child hears. It is sometimes thought that since children this age are generally unable to speak, it is not important that they be exposed to a great deal of language and talking. Actually, a very important factor in the development of the child's intelligence is exposure to language during the second year of life. Parents should talk to the child as much as possible even if it is a one-sided conversation. Certainly, it is not expected that the child will understand everything that is said, but he is learning that these big people who take care of him spend a great deal of time making sounds with their mouths. He will attempt to imitate this noise and he should be encouraged to babble and make all kinds of sounds. By continually naming the objects in the child's environment—for example, shoes, bottle, cup, the names of his toys, and the parts of his body — he will come to associate and connect particular sounds with particular objects. These associations and connections require considerable mental exercise and effort for the young child. Learning to make associations and connections between words and objects and ideas is a very important part of intellectual growth. Parents play a critical and major role in assisting their children to engage in this mental exercise, and it doesn't require any additional time to do this. Talking to your preschool child, whatever his age, is very important. The habits you develop with your one- and two-year-old will continue during his development.

A wide variety of physical activities is also important during the second year. The child is beginning to walk and this greatly expands his ability to explore. He has a lot to learn about the world around him, and he should be encouraged to explore. Rather than restrict a child in a playpen, it is better to encourage him to gain mastery over his body by allowing him to explore and move around the house. Of course at this point, it is also important to childproof the rooms in which the child can roam. In short, this means removing all objects of danger to the child, or which you wouldn't want to have broken.

Small muscle activity is also very important. An example of an activity that one-year-old children often enjoy and one that helps to develop eye-hand coordination is putting small objects into containers. This activity helps the child learn about the things in his world and requires mental exercise. By finding out that some objects fit into others, he is learning that things can be organized into sequences and that size is relative. Some other activities that help develop a child's eye-hand corrdination are building towers with large blocks and scribbling on paper with a pencil or crayons. Again these activities require mental activity and help a child to develop his intellectual power.

The third year of a child's life, between the ages of two and three, can be one of the most important for him in terms of developing his ability to learn quickly and easily. During this period, the child's vocabulary and his ability to use sentences to communicate increase dramatically. Again it is important for the parent to help him learn the names of objects, such as big, yellow, Susan's, broken, little, and hundreds of others. He is also learning words that are used to describe actions. Books can play an important part in a child's language development during this period. Particularly useful are books that describe activities and objects with which the child has had first-hand experience. Reading these storybooks to the two-year-old is very good for him.

The two-year-old should be taught about geometric shapes, such as the circle, square, and triangle, and about colors. There are hundreds of examples of these shapes and colors in the child's environment—square doors, red chairs, etc. The clever parent takes advantage of the opportunity to acquaint his child with these different shapes and colors as he goes about his normal daily routine. This is helpful to the child in several ways. First, it helps sharpen his perception and awareness of objects in his world. It helps him to discriminate between objects in his surroundings, and this helps him to begin to classify and order his surroundings. One important part of intelligence is knowing how to classify and order things, e.g., different kinds of dogs are still part of the group called dogs, but cats are not. This requires considerable mental activity and is a very good exercise for the child's developing brain. When new things are presented to the child to learn, it is best to teach them in very small steps. For example, look at the following two attempts to teach color identification to a child.

> ***Parent No. 1: "Look Joey, here's a red truck and a white block, and a blue ball, and a pink top. Which one is blue?"***
> ***Parent No. 2: "Joey, here is a black truck and here is a white truck. This truck is black. This truck is white. Where is the black truck?"***

The method used by Parent No. 2 is more likely to be successful than the method used by Parent No. 1. Who can tell me why?

> ***Pause for response. (Correct responses: fewer colors involved, easier discrimination required, objects differ only in color.) Be sure to get or supply all three responses.***

For most children the easiest colors to learn are black and white and then red, yellow, and blue.

The two-year-old is also beginning to develop the idea that numbers represent the order of things. It is both easy and important for a parent to help his child understand the concept of numbers. The first thing is for him to learn the names of numbers one through ten. Again, this can be done in the normal routine of the household.

Q. What are some ways counting can be used by the parent in the normal household routine?

> ***Pause for responses. The idea is to elicit responses consisting of items the parent can count with the child. Examples include silverware, toys, chimes, etc. Perhaps the best method in terms of getting parents to be aware of counting is to get into the habit of counting steps when helping a child up and down them. Suggest this to parents if it is not volunteered as a response.***

Very good! You are coming up with ways in which your home can be an interesting learning environment for a young child.

For the child between the ages of three and four, it is important to expand on the exercises and ideas presented earlier, such as shape, color, and number. The three-year-old is beginning to understand the meaning of numbers now and can go beyond counting. He can begin to answer questions about "how many" and should be given frequent opportunities to do this. He is also capable of learning the alphabet and learning to recognize and identify letters. Many opportunities are present within the home for him to engage in saying and identifying letters. Probably the best letters to start with are the letters in his name. Also it is somewhat confusing at first to learn capital and lower case letters at the same time, so stick to just one at first. Magnetic letters stuck to the refrigerator provide easy and frequent access for the three-year-old and remind the parents to engage in play activities with their child centered around the identification of letters.

Particularly helpful in providing both instruction for the child and suggestions for the parent about what kind of activities are useful are educational television shows such as "Sesame Street." For example, one activity which is part of every "Sesame Street" program involves the child in examining the ways objects are alike and different. These activities make the child aware of how things are alike and different. This mental exercise forms one of the basic methods of reasoning. There are many occasions during the day to help your child with this exercise. For example, we can show the child three or four pieces of clothing and ask how they are alike. Or, the parent could show the child several blue objects and one red one and ask the child to find which one doesn't belong or which one is different. So you can see that educational television programs have educational value both for the child and for the parent. They can be the source of many ideas on how to exercise your child's brain.

OPTIONAL   The three-year-old can also engage in other worthwhile activities which are not as easily seen to be of educational value. For example, it is extremely important that the child be encouraged to play different roles, such as doctor, nurse, teacher, mother, father, big brother, husband, wife, etc. Educators are beginning to realize that such activities are extremely important for the developing intellect. They require the child to step out of his own mind temporarily and assume the thoughts and actions of someone else. This is difficult mental activity. It not only requires a great deal of mental effort, but helps the child to develop sufficient mental flexibility to perfect his performance of various roles. The most important thing that parents can do to assist the child in his play is to play right along with him. And be sure to let him decide who plays what role. He can learn a good deal about how to pretend well by watching you pretend well and play your part well. Again such activities are very stimulating for a child's intelligence and he is highly motivated to perform the various roles.

Another important mental activity for the three-year-old which can also have a strong play quality to it involves stimulating the child to utilize his memory. Frequent questions about what happened yesterday or last week or when he visited grandmother will help to develop skill in remembering. One parent used the following game to exercise his child's memory. The child had a box of small, plastic animals. Several were selected and the parent asked the child, for example, to put the lion on his bed. When the child returned, he was asked to put the giraffe on the television and so on until several had been hidden. Then the child was asked to find the lion or find the giraffe. He had to remember where he had put each animal and was obviously delighted when he remembered correctly. Again, it is important to set up this game in small steps, starting with two animals at first, to insure that the child meets with success. Encouraging a child to utilize his memory helps to develop his intelligence.

With the four-year-old, further developing his skill in the areas already described will occupy a great deal of the parent's effort in stimulating the child's intelligence. Helping him to increase his verbal skills again should be emphasized. The four-year-old is able to describe things that happen in fairly good detail and should be encouraged to do this. He spends more time thinking about how others think and feel. By age six, he is likely to know most of the letters in the alphabet by sight and can write any of them on request. He can also begin to associate letters with the sound they make and many games can be developed to help promote the skill. For example, the parent can say to the child: "I am thinking of a color that starts with the letter **R**," or the game could be taking turns naming words that begin with the letter **P**.

In all of the activities we have discussed, it is not helpful to associate the child's age with his performance on a certain task. It is more important to think in terms of the sequence of tasks involved and to concentrate on getting from one to the next in the proper sequence. Think of the sequence of tasks involved in the child's being able to name words that start with the letter **P**. First, he has to be able to distinguish between different sounds; at first loud and soft, then **sss** and **puh**, and then **buh** and **puh**. Next, he has to learn the names of letters, and then he has to learn that different letters make different sounds. And finally, he has to be able to produce the sound that **P** makes and think of words that begin with the **P** sound. So there is a whole series of tasks and again, the ages at which each task is learned is not as important as is building from one step to the next. You will each receive a small booklet describing sequences of exercises designed to develop your child's intelligence. Remember, the next step in the sequence is what counts and not your child's age.

We've briefly mentioned during this session a lot of activities that will help a young child develop his intellectual potential to the fullest. Of course this session hasn't directly helped the child, but I hope it has helped stimulate your curiosity and has given you some ideas to use with young children. In the last few minutes, let's provide some practice in catching the opportunities to help a young child develop his intelligence. Here is a situation. Suppose you have a two-and-one-half-year-old son and you are in the grocery store.

Q. What might you do to help stimulate his intelligence; that is, to make the experience a learning experience?

   Pause for responses. Many are acceptable.

Very good. Now suppose you want to teach the ideas of relationships such as "on," "in," "under," and "next to."

Q. How do you do that?

   Pause for responses.

Q. How could you teach your eighteen-month-old about big and little?

   Pause for responses.

Very good. Remember there are many, many opportunities for instruction throughout the child's day. In part, how intelligent your child will be depends on how well you take advantage of the opportunities you have to exercise your child's mind during the routine of your daily activities.

   Optional epilogue, as follows:

   In closing I would like to make one important point. Research has demonstrated that children who don't go to nursery schools do just as well as or better than the average child who goes to nursery school before he starts school if the child's parents take an active role in the child's preschool development in the home. The volume **Your Child's Intellect** by T.H. Bell (Olympus Publications) is an excellent guide to home-based preschool instruction.

   This is a good time to have parents examine homemade and commercial educational toys, as well as the book Your Child's Intellect. *During this informal portion of the session, the parents should be encouraged to share ideas. You can help by clarifying parents' developmental expectations of their children. If this lesson is given as a single presentation, it is helpful to give as a handout the Criteria for Toy Selection, which is at the back of the Parent Workbook. The criteria may also be used to stimulate discussion by having parents read it and ask questions.*

21

SPECIAL EDUCATION

Objectives

1. To help parents understand that exceptionality refers to any child who deviates far enough from the norm that special educational services are required.
2. To help parents recognize that there is no absolute norm that applies to all individuals and that there are vast differences in physical, maturational, and psychological development of all children.
3. To help parents appreciate the different areas of special education by presenting the range of various handicaps to the learning process.
4. To introduce various educational provisions for the placement of exceptional children.

Materials

1. Blackboard
2. Chalk
3. Eraser

I would like to begin today's meeting by telling you a true story of a twenty-three-year-old shoe clerk named Bill. His employer considers Bill one of the best employees he's ever had. Bill is not only very dependable and hard working, but extremely courteous and pleasant to the customers as well. Every day Bill comes into the store on time, greets his employer and other salespersons with a friendly smile and "Good morning," and begins his work. Because he has difficulty with the paper work — adding figures on the sales receipts — he always uses an adding machine. He performs his duties of waiting on customers, exchanging small talk, finding their correct shoe size, and stocking the shelves without any difficulty. It is obvious that he enjoys the work from his readiness to perform and his friendly appearance.

This may not sound like an unusual or even interesting story, but let me tell you where the story began. Bill started school when he was six years old and appeared to be slightly behind the other children in his class. His teacher, Miss Jacobs, didn't consider it too unusual, as many children have difficulty when they first begin school. It is a much different kind of experience than they have been used to and there are a number of adjustments to make. He made friends quite easily and treated his teacher with courtesy and respect. However, toward mid-year, his classwork was much behind the others in his grade. He was, at this point, just beginning to do the work his classmates had done at the beginning of school, four months earlier. The teacher was concerned about Bill and convinced that his difficulty had nothing to do with his encountering a new situation, as she had once suspected. From talking with Bill's mother on the phone, visiting with her at home, and from his good social interactions, it was apparent that he enjoyed school. Because of her interest in Bill's welfare, she consulted with his parents and they agreed to let the school psychologist interview him and administer some tests. During the testing, Bill was very friendly and showed much interest in the questions, puzzles, and "games" the psychologist used in evaluating him. He did not tire and was enthusiastic throughout the testing situation.

The psychologist's report indicated that Bill was intellectually retarded. He would always work slightly behind his peers because his potential is lower than the majority of children his age. The psychologist recommended that Bill be placed in a new class that had begun a year ago at the school. It was a special education class for the mentally retarded. A teacher trained at the graduate level in mental retardation had been employed. She received special training in working with children who are retarded. Special materials are used with these children in order to help them learn with a minimum of frustration and failure.

Bill was an exceptional child. He had the advantage of being identified early and a program of treatment was specifically designed to fit his needs. Bill probably would have failed in school and later in a job, but his parents and the school did certan things that benefitted him. With proper schooling, Bill learned to function socially and occupationally. Although his ability to do school work is much below average, he is a responsible, contributing adult.

Pause.

If we are to understand people, we must learn that there is no such thing as a normal or a normal standard that applies to all individuals. From the earliest times it has been recognized that everyone will vary in some way from what might be called "normal" in terms of physical characteristics and psychological development. Height is a good example; look at the different sizes of people in this room. Most often the differences are small. However, sometimes the differences are so big that they require some changes to allow the person to get along: for example, a short person may drive a car by sitting on a cushion; a very tall man — say 6′9″ — may have door arches made higher in his house; he may not drive a Volkswagen, but he still can drive another car.

Treating all children as if they were alike in capability and in intelligence is the same as dressing all children in the same size clothes. Even though differences in mental ability can have some affect in the area of social adjustment, they are as natural as differences in height.

The exceptional child is a child who doesn't and cannot learn by the ordinary methods of teaching used in a regular classroom. The exceptional child can learn if a special education program is provided. Now special education programs are not all the same; what will be required depends on the child's handicaps. In some instances, a special class, separate from the regular classroom, will be needed. In other instances the child will spend most of his time in a regular classroom, but will need special educational tutoring; in still other instances the child may stay in a regular classroom if the teacher is provided with special materials and weekly guidance concerning how to teach the child.

Now before we consider some of the different kinds of exceptional children, I would like to make a very important point. We must always remember that the exceptional child is first of all a child. This means that he needs love, understanding, and security that all children need to grow. The exceptional child may have some limitations, but to emphasize these and think of the child in terms of his limitations is unfair. As parents or teachers, we must always think of the child with needs to succeed, to please, to be accepted, and to accept himself. Secondly, we must find ways to make these things happen at home and in the classroom.

The people of the United States have always recognized the importance of eduation. In every state children are required by law to attend school until sixteen or seventeen years of age. The exceptional child must also attend, but if the school is to be productive, for him special programs must be provided, and this will require specially trained teachers, special materials such as braille paper, buses with a chair lift, school buildings with ramps instead of steps, to name just a few of the needed changes. Yet is is expensive for communities to provide this special education, but it is even more expensive not to provide this education. If the exceptional child is made self-supporting, which is possible in 90 percent of the cases, then the taxpayers won't have to keep paying for this child as an adult through welfare or by institutionalization. Remember Bill the shoe salesman. In 1980 he earned $8,600 per year and paid his taxes like everyone else. If Bill were on welfare or institutionalized, taxpayers would have paid between $20,000-$25,000 per year to support him. In short, providing exceptional children with special education is not only the humane thing to do, it is also good business.

Now let's consider some of the characteristics of the most common groups of exceptional children who are found in the public schools. We will look at the mentally retarded, emotionally disturbed, and the learning disabled child. The characteristics and needs of the physically handicapped, visually impaired, and hearing-impaired child are fairly obvious.

Write on board: Mentally retarded.

The mentally retarded child has a slower rate of learning than other children. This means that it takes him much longer than the rest of his class to learn his schoolwork and he will need many more reviews of the same information. Since the mentally retarded learn at a slower rate, they also mature socially at a slower rate. However, if provided the kind of education and support with which Bill our shoe salesman was provided, many of these children can by adulthood (age twenty-one to twenty-five) be self-supporting, independent, and socially adjusted. Remember the only unique characteristic of the retarded child is his slower rate of learning; his capacity for love, kindness, loyalty, and every other important human quality is there to be developed just as it is in all children.

The characteristics of the emotionally disturbed child are much more complicated and varied than most of the other exceptional conditions.

Write on board: Emotionally disturbed.

The emotionally disturbed child may show any one or more of the following behaviors:

1. Extreme aggression and deliberate destruction of property.
2. Fearful, tense, and nervous.
3. Frequently argumentative with parents, teachers, or friends and often unhappy.
4. Frequent physical problems, e.g. headaches, stomachaches.
5. Usually very shy and withdrawn, often lives in a world of daydreams.

Now all children show these behaviors from time to time; there are two important factors that determine whether the child is emotionally disturbed. The first is how severe the problem is and the second is how often the behavior occurs. It is not uncommon for a child to become withdrawn, sad, and depressed for a few days, for example following the death of a favorite pet, or in some cases to become angry, aggressive and destructive. However, when this condition lasts for a month or more, then professional help is needed. The emotionally disturbed child often behaves in ways that are upsetting to adults and other children, and therefore these children don't get the sympathy and understanding they need. As a point of fact, the natural and normal responses of adults to children who are emotionally disturbed tend to make the problems worse. The classroom teacher is not a psychologist or psychiatrist, but if such personnel are available on a weekly basis to discuss the management of the child, many disturbed children can be both educated and treated for their disturbance in a regular classroom. In some instances, however, a separate classroom is needed. The emotionally disturbed child, when treated properly, can learn up to his ability and can be a productive and responsible adult.

Write on board: Learning disabled.

The learning disabled child is a child with average or above average intelligence who has a specific problem or set of problems that interfere with his learning some school-related skills such as arithmetic, reading, listening, or writing. In some instances these children may do very well in most areas but are very weak in others; for example, a fourth-grade learning disabled child may do fifth-grade arithmetic but may be unable to read; or he may be able to spell at a first-grade level and read at a fifth-grade level. These children are obviously not retarded, yet in some areas they don't learn with the usual methods of teaching. They need a special-education program. Frequently, these children have problems in expressing their knowledge and interpreting what they take in from their senses. Let me give you some examples of how these problems operate. The learning disabled child may, when reading, interpret words such as "no" for "on," or "dog" for God"; he may write 69 for 96 or 35 for 53; he may read or write a "b" for a "d" or a "p" for a "q." While reversals of letters and numbers are not uncommon up to age 7 or 8, by the time a child is 9 years of age these difficulties are very suggestive of a learning disability.

Some children are unable to tell the difference between similar sounds. This will prevent them from learning to read using phonetics. For example, they cannot tell the difference between short *a* and *e*, or *ch* and *sh.* Some children are unable to focus their attention and are hyperactive, distractable, or slow and dazed-like. Poor fine and/or gross motor coordination problems are also frequently associated with learning disability problems. However, we should remember never to be quick to do our own diagnosing. This is an area that requires the skills of trained specialists. It is important to note that this issue is often clouded by many other factors and it is a rare child who manifests only one problem or symptom.

When provided special instruction, either by a tutor, the regular classroom teacher with proper materials, or in a special class, these children usually are able to return to a regular classroom in two or three years. These children usually learn ways of getting around their problem and compensating for it.

Now let's consider how an exceptional child is usually identified. You will note from what I say that a wide variety of specialists need to be available. To begin our understanding of this process, let's consider a common case. Jim is a third-grade child who is failing the third grade. In fact, he has failed both first and second grades and reads on a beginning first-grade level. In addition, Jim is always being a clown and frequently being sent to the principal's office. Jim's first-grade teacher just thought he was slow. His second-grade teacher thought he was just a spoiled child who needed a good spanking, and his third-grade teacher doesn't know what to think since she sees lots of conflicting evidence. This teacher made a referral to the school psychologist and visiting teachers who began the diagnostic process. The process may involve testing; interviewing parents, child and teacher; observation of the child; and tentative changes in the work presented to the child. With the results of the evaluation, a treatment program is developed, directed at the problem behavior observed by the teacher and, if possible, at any known causes of the problem. In Jim's case the psychologist determined that Jim was not retarded and that he had above average intelligence. However, Jim had both visual and an auditory discrimination problem. This means he often cannot tell the difference between similar sounds that he hears and similar shapes that he sees. Well, these abilities are very important to reading. The psychologist also noted that Jim was well liked by his classmates and his gym teacher, and the other adults in the school described him as a cooperative child. The visiting teacher found that Jim's parents were concerned about his failing in school, and they described him as a happy cooperative child. However, the visiting teacher did learn that when he was frustrated or failing at something, he would act dumb and silly, which was quite upsetting to Jim's parents. From this and other information it was obvious that Jim was not retarded, not spoiled and not emotionally disturbed, although he might become disturbed with time if his problem were to go untreated.

Jim was diagnosed as having a learning disability and the services of a resource teacher would be needed. The resource teacher would see Jim for 20 minutes each day and work with him on exercises aimed at overcoming his problem. The resource teacher would also help Jim's regular classroom teacher by providing any special materials needed in the regular classroom. The school psychologist would work with Jim's teacher to help Jim give up his self-destructive, silly behavior. Incidentally this behavior made good sense; what would you do if you were a child who couldn't do what people asked? Jim found acting silly got him sent out of the room and that meant relief from the frustration of trying to do work he couldn't do without special help.

Today we took a look at exceptional children and special education. I would like to leave you with these ideas:

First, all children, whether exceptional or not, are first of all children and have the same needs for love, understanding, social contact, and achievement.

Second, special education is not one thing, it involves many different specialists, methods, materials, and programs. If your child or a friend's child is to be placed in a special education program, it should be specific and should be fully explained to the parents.

Third, the problems and needs of exceptional children are real and in many instances curable or correctable. As all children, these children need the adult community to ensure that their needs are met, and this means making sure your schools have available the special education programs needed by the children of your community.

I recognize that what was presented here today was primarily in the form of a lecture and it might be helpful for all of us if we could take some time to share our reactions and our experiences with special education.

    Pause.

Q. Would anyone care to share their reactions?

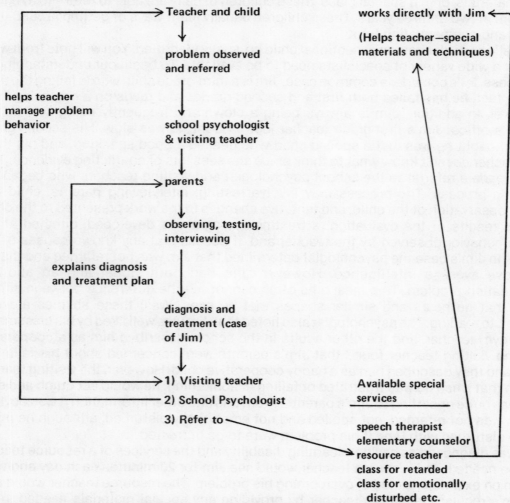

Illustrative Handling of a Child with Learning and Behavior Problems

22

HELPING YOUR CHILD WITH HIS SCHOOLWORK

Objectives

1. To teach parents how to decide whether their child needs tutoring, and if so, what he should be tutored in.
2. To teach parents how to go about tutoring their child.

Materials

1. Blackboard
2. Chalk
3. Eraser
4. Paper and pencils

INTRODUCTION   Many children have difficulty with at least one subject during the elementary school years. Although teachers try to give each child the individual attention and extra help needed to get through these difficult periods, it is sometimes impossible for them to provide all the individual help required. So, sometimes the responsibility for providing extra help rests with the parents. This extra, individual help can be called tutoring. With tutoring, two questions are very important. One is what should you tutor your child on? The other question is how do you tutor?

The question of the content of tutoring must be decided in conference with your child's teacher. Generally, the problem areas in the early school years are reading and math. The specific skills to be taught in the tutoring sessions should be arrived at by discussing your child's progress with his teacher. This ensures not only that the tutoring sessions cover the skills of most importance, but also lets the teacher know that you are interested in and concerned about your child's progress.

It is very important that you approach your child's teacher with a positive and constructive attitude. Unfortunately, parents are often so unhappy about their child falling behind that they either directly or indirectly blame their child's teachers and act aggressive or annoyed toward them. Nearly all teachers take a personal interest in their pupils, and frankly, most are upset when children fall behind or fail in school. Constructive concern on the part of the parent is best shown by a relaxed inquiry about their child's performance; this will almost always produce a helpful response from your child's teachers.

Since the answer to the question of what to tutor depends on the particular child and teacher, we will not concentrate on that important part of tutoring during this session. Instead, we will concentrate on the how. That is, how to be helpful tutor.

SETTING THE EMOTIONAL TONE OF THE SESSION   There is much more to tutoring than simply knowing the correct answers to the questions. Children generally require tutoring because they are failing some subject or because they have not learned some specific skill, such as dividing words into syllables. Failing in school often causes a number of negative and disruptive behaviors to develop in children. These behaviors often cause problems in the feelings between teacher or tutor and the child. Let's look at some of these effects by looking at examples from tutoring sessions.

> ### Example No. 1:
> *Johnny sat down and his father said: "Let's look at some of those subtraction*

problems." Johnny rearranged his seat and dropped his pencil. When he picked it up he said: "Tommy and his Dad are going fishing Saturday, think we could go?"

Q. How would you describe Johnny's behavior? What would you say he is doing?

Pause for response. (Answer: Avoiding math.)

Right, Johnny is avoiding the math problems. It is very natural to want to avoid something you have failed in the past, and this something the parent-tutor will have to work on. Here is another example.

Example No. 2:
"Gee, Mom, I'll never learn to read. I'm just dumb. I'm really a failure."

In this example the child is very clear about his reaction to failure. He has met with failure in learning to read, so he has decided that he is not intelligent and is a failure as a person.

Optional:
Explain that, incidentally, this is a good example of one of the common self-defeating ideas talked about in an earlier session. Ask if anyone can identify it. Then pause for response. (Answer: judging your value as a person on the basis of your accomplishments and having to succeed in all endeavors in order to be self-accepting is just hurting yourself.)

Let's look at one more fairly common reaction to failure which might be found in a tutoring session.

Example No. 3:
Parent: "OK, Tanya, let's see what the trouble seems to be in math."
Tanya: "Oh, I can do math. It's just that old creep, Mrs. Pumpernickel. She just picks on me because I have more friends than her pet Janie does."

Q. How is Tanya handling her experience with failure?

Pause for response. (Answer: She is blaming teacher for her own shortcomings. Also demonstrates the irrational idea that since she doesn't like Mrs. Pumpernickel, she is going to do less than her best to "show her.")

As you can see, the job of tutor can be complicated first of all by the fact that children's feelings are often involved in their performance. How does the tutor handle this? We shall see as we describe the steps involved in tutoring.

The first step of course is deciding that tutoring is needed. As was said before, this occurs through discussion with the child's teacher. If the teacher and parents decide that tutoring is needed, then this decision has to be told by the parents to the child. There are three helpful points to get across to the child: that you are interested in his schoolwork, that you like to see him do well, and that you would like to help him do a bit better in one specific area or skill.

Write each on blackboard under heading: Helpful points.

In talking to your child about tutoring, there are four destructive things you should avoid doing:

First, communicating the idea to your child that he is letting you down.

Second, blaming him for doing poor work.

Third, communicating that you are ashamed of him, and

Fourth, communicating that you think he is lazy.

Let's look at some statements that might be made by a parent to his child about tutoring. You tell me what is helpful or destructive about each.

Parent No. 1:

"Billy, I talked to your teacher this morning. She told me you were doing very well in arithmetic but were having some problems with spelling. Let's work something out so I can help you with that spelling for a little while."

Q. Was Billy's parent's statement helpful or destructive?

Wait for parental response.

Very good, we see Billy's parent involved all of the helpful points and none of the destructive points in his comments.

Now let's look at another parent's way of talking to his child about tutoring and her problems with her schoolwork.

Parent No. 2:

"Sarah, I was very pleased to talk to your teacher. However, I am concerned with your reading grade. I would like to help you improve your reading: You know reading is important and you are a little lazy. I am sure if you tried harder you could do better."

Q. What was helpful or destructive about Sarah's parent's comments?

(Answer: Helpful — interest in problems. Destructive — lazy, no specific area, blaming.)

OK, now let's all imagine that your child's teacher tells you that your child needs to learn how to do long division better and you decide to tutor him. Using your child's name, write down how you would tell him about the need for tutoring.

Hand out paper and pencils.
Optional: Remind parents of earlier sessions in which "reflective listening" and "sharing yourself" communication was discussed. Explain that these skills are very important to the good tutor also. Listening to a child and observing his face is every bit as important as is talking to and telling him facts and answers during tutoring.

Let's assume that you have decided to go ahead with the tutoring session and you know the specific skill or information to be taught. The next thing to consider is how to tutor. Several points are important regarding how you set up the tutoring session. They are communication, setting up tutoring sessions so that they are enjoyable and satisfying, arranging the seating of child and tutor, making the directions clear, planning the lesson in small steps that require frequent answers, looking at the child when speaking to him, attending to each problem, and if possible providing concrete objects for child to manipulate which teach the idea.

Write all these items on board.

Now let's take a close look at setting up the tutoring session.

The *first* idea was mentioned earlier. Be sure that there are open lines of communication. You can learn a great deal about your child simply by listening to him.

The *second* general consideration is ensuring that they are enjoyable and satisfying both for the parent and the child. If after the first session, you find that tutoring is unpleasant to you or your child stop immediately and go back to listening to your child. Remember, the child's initial reaction may be based on fear and the desire to avoid the pain of failure which he experienced in the past or possibly, he fears rejection by the tutor for not being able to do the work. By being accepting and making the sessions fun you can help him get over these feelings.

Third, during the sessions it is better to sit next to your child rather than across from him. This way it is easy for both of you to see the lessons and it encourages a friendlier atmosphere.

Fourth, for some children the major difficulty in the primary grades is not in mastering the subject matter but in following directions. So be sure that the directions you give are not difficult to follow and are presented slowly and clearly.

Fifth, plan the lesson in small steps that require frequent answers. This keeps the child's attention on the work and gives you a closer look at where the difficulties lie.

For example, if you are doing addition problems, present them one at a time rather than asking the child to do a page of fifteen or twenty examples at at time.

Sixth, when your child speaks to you or when you are speaking to him be sure to look at him. It is sometimes easier to see confusion and frustration than it is to hear it.

Seventh, don't skip any problems. Wait for an answer to each one. This helps the child develop the habit of working on difficult items rather than passing them by.

And *eight,* young children learn best by having concrete objects to manipulate. Allow the child to handle the materials you are working with.

This is a rather lengthy list of things to remember in developing a tutoring style, but each item is important and should be kept in mind throughout each tutoring session. Let's look more closely at just what you do when you are tutoring.

PRAISE AND CLUES   It may seem rather basic, but during tutoring only two things can happen to each question or problem. The first thing you must remember is not to lecture the child to pay better attention, or to use any sarcasm such as: "you know better than that"; "don't be a dummy." The most skilled tutors, in fact, never even use the word "no" or phrases such as "that's not it" or "that's wrong" while they are tutoring. They know how much children and others dislike the bitterness of failure.

The skilled tutor responds to a wrong answer by restating the question and supplying the child with more clues to help in getting the correct answer. After the child gets the answer correct, it is very helpful to go over the question in its original form without the clues and praise.

Let's look at some examples.

A child is to read some arithmetic problems and then solve them. The problem reads: A boy had 5 marbles in one pocket, 5 in another, and 2 firecrackers in another pocket. How many marbles did he have all together. Your child says 12. Your response should not be "no, that is wrong."

> *You would respond: "Jimmy, look at the problem and tell me how many different kinds of things the boy had in his pockets?" (Child's response: marbles and firecrackers.) "Now, how many firecrackers did he have?" (Child responds: 2). "How many marbles did he have all together?" (Child responds: 10). "Very good. Very good."*

You can see how the tutor can work so as to never say "no" or "that is wrong."

Let's look at another example. But before we do let's make a little chart so that we can remember what to do, depending on what kind of answer the child gives to our questions.

> *Write following chart on blackboard:*
> *Correct answers — Always praise*
> *Incomplete answers — Restate question and praise correct part*
> *Wrong answers — Give child additional help, clues and praise correct answer*

OK, now we all know what to do with an answer that is correct, incomplete, or wrong. Now let's look at some examples.

Example 1:
Billy is asked to say three words that rhyme with cat. He says fat and rat. Should you say: "I

said three not two"; or "Right, fat and rat rhyme with cat. That is two, this time give me three."

> *Pause for response. (Answer: second response.)*

Q. What is wrong with the first response?

> *Pause for answer. (It is too negative.)*

Example 2:
You have shown Sally a picture of a car and a train and asked her to name the letters each start with. She says: "car starts with *C* and train starts with *K*."

Q. What do you do?

> *Pause for response. (Answer: praise and reward.) Have parents supply actual wording of their praises and clues.*

Example 3:
You have asked Tony how much 3 plus 4 are and he said 9.

Q. What do you do?

> *Pause for response. (Answer: incorrect response, so give additional help such as, here are my three fingers. I add 4 of your fingers. How many do I have?) Now he says 7.*

Q. What do you do?

> *(Answer: praise.)*

Example 4:
Billy is asked to spell four words on a piece of paper. He spells them as follows: WATER, TRAIN, FAST, WULK.

Q. What would your response be to his performance?

> *Pause for parent response. (Suggested response of parent: Water spelled WATER — good. Train is spelled TRAIN.*
> *"How do you spell train, Billy?" [Child's response.]*
> *Good. Fast is spelled FAST — good. Walk is spelled WALK.*
> *"How do you spell walk, Billy?" [Child's response.] Good.)*

Very good. If you stick to this systematic program, you will find that you will be a very effective tutor. Remember, though, that these sessions should be held consistently for as long as needed and should allow for an enjoyable interchange between you and your child.

I would like to share one last idea with you that can help you be a good tutor. If you have a tape recorder available, record your tutoring sessions with your child and then listen to them at some quiet time. Keep the following questions in mind as you listen to the tape.

1. Does this sound like a happy interaction?
2. Would I like someone to talk to me like I speak to my child?
3. Am I following the rules on how to tutor?
    a. Praising every correct answer.
    b. Restating the question for incomplete answers, but praising the correct part.
    c. Giving additional help and clues for wrong answers, and praising when the child gets them correct.

> *Distributing 3x5 cards with the above rules on it might be a valuable clue to parents who would like to tutor their child. They could keep it in their hand or in front of them while they tutor.*

23

SPECIAL EDUCATION—PL 94-142
Ann Plough—University of Virginia

Objectives

1. To inform parents of the principle provisions of PL 94-142 Education for All Handicapped Children Act.
2. To describe for parents the sequence of steps followed in obtainng special educational services for a handicapped child.

Materials

1. Handout, see last page of this chapter.

Background Readings & Reverences

Weatherley, Richard A. *Reforming Special Education: Policy Implementation from State Level to Street Level.* M.I.T. Press, Cambridge, 1979.
Educating All the Handicapped: What the Laws Say & What Schools are Doing. Education U.S.A. Special Report, National School Public Relations Association, Arlington, 1977.
Hagerty, Robert & Howard, Thomas. *How to Make Federal Mandatory Special Education Work for You: A Handbook for Educators & Consumers,* Charles C. Thomas, Springfield, Ill.: 1978.
Getting Uncle Sam to Enforce Your Civil Rights. Publications Division, U.S. Commission on Civil Rights, Washington, D.C. 204 425 (202-254-6600) available free of charge, 44 pages.

In 1975 the federal government passed an educational law, which will probably affect most of your children to one extent or another before they finish high school. The law I am referring to is Public Law 94-142, the Education for All Handicapped Children Act. Tonight I would like to briefly describe PL 94-142, a law which is designed to ensure that all handicapped children have available to them a free and appropriate public education. In my discussion I will try to answer four major questions about the law. First, who are the children served by 94-142? Second, what services are made available to these children by the law? Where are these services provided? And last, how are these services obtained for a child?

Write on board: What services are made available by the law?

Public Law 94-142 states that all handicapped children should receive special education and related services designed to meet their unique needs. Examples of special needs are: a blind child who cannot see the blackboard. The teaching method must be altered accordingly. A mentally retarded youngster would benefit from small group instruction with material adjusted to his abilities. He would benefit more from vocational training than from a college preparatory curriculum. A child in a wheelchair will need ramps, elevators, and a special school bus, and an emotionally disturbed child might benefit greatly from some sort of counseling services for himself and his parents. Whatever is deemed appropriate for a handicapped child must be provided by the local school district, and it must be provided free of charge. For example, if no appropriate public education program is available for a handicapped child in his or her own school district, the local school system must provide and pay for an alternate placement as close to the child's home as possible. Also, if placement of a child in a public or private residential setting seems most appropriate, the local school district must provide the total cost of the program, including room and board.

Write on board: Where are these services provided?

According to 94-142, every handicapped child has the right to be educated in what is called the "least restrictive environment." This means that handicapped children should be placed with non-handicapped children in regular classes to the extent that this is educationally appropriate. Services should be no more intensive than necessary and only when the use of supplementary aids and resource services is not sufficient should a handicapped child be placed in a special class or a separate school.

Write on board: How are these services obtained for a handicapped child?

Every handicapped child between the age of three and twenty-one should receive a free appropriate education in the least restrictive environment. But how are these services obtained for a handicapped child? How can you, as parents, be sure that a child is being educated appropriately? I would like to illustrate the process involved with an example.

Mark Brown is 7 years old and is in the second grade. He is a cheerful, energetic youngster who enjoys running around and playing with his friends. Last year he did all right in school, he passed although he seemed a bit behind his classmates. This year, however, he is failing. His **parents are concerned** and have tried to help him at home by reading with him and going over his math work. When they work with him, Mark seems to try very hard to get things right but he just cannot do it. The Browns went to **see Mark's teacher** and found that she was also concerned about his slow progress. She decided to refer Mark to what is called an **"in-school screening committee"**. Within a few days, this committee which included the school principal and Mark's teacher met. They reviewed Mark's report cards, test scores, and school work from the past two years and decided that a more **formal assessment** of his educational needs was advisable. At this point Mr. and Mrs. Brown were notified of the committee's decision, advised of their rights, and asked to sign a paper giving **their permission for the assessment** to begin. With the Brown's consent, the local school district began a formal evaluation. Mark was seen by a school psychologist, a doctor, a special teacher, and a speech and hearing team. Each of these specialists utilized whatever tests and evaluation procedures seemed appropriate in order to determine Mark's present level of functioning. When every aspect of Mark's **evaluation was completed,** an **eligibility meeting was held.** Mark's teacher, the school psychologist, several others teachers, and the administrator of special education participated. They reviewed all of the components of the formal assessment including Mark's aptitude and achievement test scores, his teachers' recommendations and, his physical and adaptive behavior reports. After considering all of this information, the committee decided that Mark was a handicapped child. They determined he was an educable mentally retarded child, and therefore needed some sort of **special education program** to help him do his best in school. The committee decided that Mark would do well in a resource program for retarded children, 2 periods per day and at other times, e.g. lunch, recess, art, social studies, he could spend with his regular classmates. It was felt that this type of educational program was most appropriate and at the same time least restrictive for Mark.

After the eligibility meeting, a planning session was scheduled to develop what is called an *individualized education program or IEP* for Mark. The Browns were notified of the purpose, time, and location of this meeting so that they could plan to attend. The meeting was held at the elementary school and Mark's teacher, his parents, the teacher of the class for retarded children, and a local school district representative were present. All of these people worked to design an IEP for Mark. Every IEP has to include five things. These are: A statement of the child's present level of educational performance. A description of annual goals for the child, including short term teaching objectives. A statement describing the specific educational and related services to be provided for the child and the extent to which he/she will be able to participate in regular class programs, the projected dates for initiation of services and the anticipated duration of these services. And finally, a description of appropriate criteria for determining whether the teaching objectives are being achieved. All of these components were specified for Mark and then written up into the IEP. A few days later the program was implemented and Mark began to divide his day between the resource classes for retarded children and his regular class. In the resource class he received some individual attention and specialized instruction. However, he still saw his friends during art, social studies, PE, lunch, and recess.

After spending a year in this special classroom, Mark's IEP was reviewed and updated. The resource class still seemed most appropriate and Mark was again placed in this program. In two more years another formal assessment or "re-evaluation" will be done to determine the most appropriate and least restrictive educational environment for Mark.

Pause.

The process by which special services are obtained for a handicapped child is very extensive. It involves four major stages. First, a child is referred to the in-school screening committee by his/her teacher or parents. Here the child's educational records are reviewed, If the committee suspects that a child is handicapped, the formal assessment process is begun. At this point the parents must be notified in their native language of what is going on with their child and their written informed consent must be obtained. Once parental permission is secured, the formal evaluation of a child can begin. This assessment generally includes educational, sociological, medical, and psychological components. Any tests which are used in the evaluation must be administered to the child in his/her native language or other mode of communication and must be racially and culturally non-discriminatory. After the evaluation is complete, the specialists involved meet for an eligibility meeting. Here they attempt to specify the child's present skill levels and his/her need for special education and related services. After the eligibility meeting, stage three begins in which the child's individualized educational program is developed. Parental participation is encouraged in the process of designing a unique program for the child. Once the IEP is written, the fourth stage begins and services specified in the child's IEP are delivered. Each year the child's IEP is reviewed and if it seems necessary to continue special education services, the IEP is rewritten. If the child remains in special education services, the IEP is rewritten. If the child remains in special education, a formal evaluation is conducted every three years.

Throughout this process parental involvement is encouraged. Parents should be told exactly what is happening with their child and they should have access to the school records kept on their child at all times. If at any time they become concerned about the services being provided for their child they have the right to obtain an independent evaluation or to schedule an independent hearing.

Pause.

Tonight I have spent quite a bit of time describing Public Law 94-142, The Education for All Handicapped Children Act. I would like to use the rest of the time we have to answer any questions you might have about this law and it's implicatons within our school system.

ASSISTANCE GUIDELINES
Consumer Concerns & Complaints Regarding Handicapped Children

Two major federal laws and agencies which may be of help (P.L. 94-142 & Public Law 93-112, Section 504). Typical complaints might include that the child: was not adequately assessed, was not provided an Individual Education Plan, did not receive a needed related service, or was not afforded an impartial hearing.

Parents should first make their concerns known to the Director of Special Education for their local school system. Only after efforts at the local leval have been unsuccessful should the following procedures be used.

Complaints should be addressed to either the Office of New Programs, Office for Civil Rights, HEW, Washington, D.C. 20201 or the Bureau of Education for the Handicapped, 400 Maryland Avenue, Donohoe Building, Washington, D.C. 20202. The complaint should be as brief as possible but should include the following:

1. Name, address, and phone number of the person making the complaint.
2. Name, address, and phone number of the person who has been the victim of the discrimination or inappropriate program.
3. A description of the individual's handicap.
4. The name and address of the program (school, institution, facility) that caused the discrimination or inappropriate program. (Note: The program must receive federal funds in order for Section 504 to give you protection.)
5. A description of the problem and the dates involved.
6. A description of your attempt to solve the problem, (a local hearing, a letter to the state educational agency) and what happened as a result of these efforts.

Sign and date the complaint and attach copies (not the originals) of any relevant correspondence about this problem.

Your complaint will be referred to the HEW regional office for investigation. You will be contacted by an investigator for further information and the school or facility will be asked for its side of the story. If your complaint is accurate and the school is not in compliance, HEW has the authority of require compliance.

WARNING!!

Any complaint should not be filed just as a means of harrassing a school or agency. But if the school or agency will no longer talk to the parents about their child's situation, and the parents honestly feel there is a violation, a complaint will force the school or agency to confront the issue and either produce facts to back up its position or change its practice.

Other Assistance Sources:

Children's Defense Fund
1520 New Hampshire Ave., N.W.
Washington, D.C. 20036
(202) 483-1470

Center for Law & Education Inc.
Gutman Library
6 Appian Way
Cambridge, Massachusetts 02138
(617) 495-4666

National Center for Law & the Handicapped Inc.
211 W. Washington St., Suite 1900
South Bend, Indiana 46601
(219) 288-4751

24

COMMUNICATING EFFECTIVELY WITH YOUR CHILD'S TEACHERS

Sherry Kraft
University of Virginia

Objectives

1. To help parents conduct effective parent-teacher conferences.
2. To increase parents' understanding of underlying feelings that affect the behavior of both parents and teachers in the conferences.

I am often surprised by how little information parents have about their child's experiences at school. Usually the information they do have comes from letter and number grades on report cards and the books and papers which the child brings home. Parents and teachers often don't have any direct communications. In fact, many parents feel quite uncomfortable about contacting their child's teacher and anxious if the teacher calls to request a meeting. For many parents, these feelings may be related to the fact that, for many of them, the "teacher" is still associated with their own childhood, when the teacher was a strong authority figure who defined what was right and wrong and who judged them. Therefore, relating to their child's teacher on an equal basis may require a great deal of effort to understand the teacher's role and the reasons why the teacher may feel that a conference with the parents is important. Parents also need to realize that teachers often come to parent-teacher conferences with their own apprehensions and uncertainties about how they will be viewed by the child's parents. Understanding the perspective of the teacher, as well as the feelings that you as a parent may bring to the parent-teacher conference, will help to make your relationship with the teacher not only productive but enjoyable as well.

PURPOSES OF THE PARENT-TEACHER CONFERENCE

Many parents hold the belief that parent-teacher conferences occur for only two reasons: (a) their child is behaving badly or (b) their child is having serious problems keeping up with schoolwork. While these reasons are accurate for some conferences, they are not the only conditions in which conferences occur. In fact, conferences may serve quite a variety of functions, and we will review five of them:

1. *To report on the child's progress.* Sometimes teachers want to inform parents more personally and directly about their child's overall performance at school. In this type of conference, the parent can expect to hear both strengths and weaknesses of their child's performance, as well as how their child is doing in relation to his or her level of ability.

2. *To compare their (teacher's) understanding of the child with that of the parents.* Sometimes the teacher may notice something in the child's behavior which could be of concern. However, before deciding that a problem exists, or what it is, the teacher may want to find out how the parents view the problem. There are three important reasons for the teacher to do this: (a) the parents have known the child for longer than the teacher and are much more familiar with the typical behavior of their child. It is impor-

tant for the teacher to know whether the child has behaved this way in other classroom and home situations or whether something specific to this classroom is contributing to the child's behavior. (b) The teacher may be misreading the child's behavior, for example, interpreting quietness as lack of interest. (c) It is helpful for the teacher to know whether the child has been behaving this way for a long time, or whether something has happened recently which may be affecting the child's performance temporarily—for example, the death of a grandparent or other family member, separation or divorce of the parents. What the teacher is looking for in this type of conference is (a) *feedback* from the parents about whether their way of understanding their child fits with those of the teacher, (b) an *explanation* of factors that may be affecting the child's behavior and (c) *suggestions* from the parents about helpful ways of relating to the child in the classroom. The teacher usually will begin this type of conference with an open-ended comment such as "Joey seems to get very anxious about finishing all his work. Do you notice this at home too?"

3. ***To ask parents for specific help.*** A child may be having difficulties with schoolwork which are related to what the child does at home. Therefore, the teacher may need assistance to help the child overcome this difficulty. In this type of conference, the teacher has two goals: (a) to inform the parents about the child's difficulty and (b) to solicit parents' help in resolving the difficulty. For example, the teacher may open the meeting by stating "Cindy seems to be having trouble getting her homework done. I wonder if we could work out some ways you could help her with this at home." If parents are uncertain about how to best help their child, the teacher usually can offer specific suggestions and strategies.

The types of special education services offered by the schools and steps involved in the referal process are described more fully in chapter ??.

5. ***Parent Initiated Conferences.*** As parents also may request conferences with their child's teacher, it is important to remember that many teachers are overworked and have larger than desired classes to cope with. The result is that they may be able to attend only to some of the problems and needs of children in their classes. Scheduling regular contact with parents of all their children may be extremely difficult to accomplish; therefore parents may need to take the initiative to schedule conferences if they have specific questions or if they want to know generally how their child is doing.

THE PARENTS' PERSPECTIVE: COMMON FEELINGS PARENTS BRING TO A CONFERENCE

As mentioned previously, some of the feelings parents have toward their child's teacher may come from their own experience as a child. As a result, parents may feel that they, not the child, are being judged or graded. Just being aware of this possibility can help parents separate these feelings from the reality of the equal relationship they now have with their child's teacher.

We will review eight of the common negative and positive feelings which parents experience in relation to their child's teacher. These include:

1. ***Guilt:*** "If I were a better parent, my child wouldn't have problems." Parents often blame themselves, although they most likely cannot identify things which relate directly to the child's difficulties. Such guilt feelings may actually complicate the situation, since they may lead parents to focus on themselves and not enough on the teacher's communications and their child's immediate needs.

2. ***Guilt:*** "If I were more involved with my child's schoolwork, my child wouldn't have problems." A similar type of self-blame may be experienced by parents who are very busy. They may believe that other parents devote more time to their children's school-

work and that their own child, therefore, is at a disadvantage. These feelings may make it difficult for the parents to allow their child to receive outside help.

3. *Fear:* "The teacher will talk about things I don't understand." Most parents have not had much contact with schools in several years. Many of the methods and materials used in schools have changed. Parents may find themselves unfamiliar with the ideas and methods used in their child's classroom. While this lack of familiarity is normal and to be expected, parents often become quite uncomfortable. The discomfort parents feel may be made worse by a teacher who uses professional jargon and terms which parents are unfamiliar with. Rather than asking questions or asking for further explanations, parents may sit through the conference in uncomfortable and confused silence, which results in little communication and understanding.

4. *Fear:* "The teacher will find out all the things I'm doing wrong as a parent." Some parents believe that teachers know not only the right answers to the child's homework, but also the right approaches and methods to be used in all situations with a child. Parents mistakenly may believe that the teacher feels confident and in control at all times. They fear that the parent-teacher conference will expose their flaws, and they may actively avoid contact with the teacher for this reason. In such cases, their child's needs may remain undiscovered because of the parents' own anxieties and fears.

5. *Resentment:* "I don't have time to solve my child's school problems along with everything else. Why don't they just do their job?" Given the pressures of work, household management and other family needs, parents may understandably wish to leave their child's educational needs and concerns in the hands of school personnel who they see as experts. While the schools are responsible for each child's education, part of a parent's responsibility includes keeping informed about their child's progress. Since parents have the most experience with the particular characteristics of their child, their input and assistance may be necessary for teachers to be able to work effectively with a child. When parents feel resentment toward teachers for requesting their involvement, they frequently are reacting to the stress and pressure in their own life. Understanding the reasons for their reactions may enable the parents to respond more positively to a specific request from the teacher.

6. *Fear:* "They'll tell me my child has terrible problems I didn't even know about!" These feelings stem from inaccurate beliefs or myths that parents may hold—for example, that behavior problems are indicative of mental illness or that learning problems mean that a child is brain damaged. Such ideas are frightening to parents, and this fear may lead to an avoidance of the teacher or to problems recognizing that the child is having difficulties.

Fortunately, a parent-teacher conference may evoke more positive feelings in addition to, or instead of, the fear, guilt, and resentment described above. These may include:

7. *Relief:* "At last someone is interested in getting my opinion!" Many parents have expressed frustration at the attitude of some professionals who work with children. Unfortunately, professionals too often act as though parents have no expertise or understanding of their child's needs or problems. These professionals show little interest in discussing the situation with the parents or responding to the parents' questions. For many parents, therefore, an interested, concerned teacher who wants to include their perspective in meeting the child's needs is a refreshing and welcome change.

8. *Curiosity:* "I've been wondering what my child's school experience is really like." After the first few years of life, children are increasingly influenced by people and events outside the realm of home and family. A child's relationship with a teacher can have significant impact on the development of self-image and confidence and can affect the child's behavior at home. Many parents find that getting to know their teachers and learning about the school environment can help them understand and appreciate their child's behavior and development.

THE TEACHER'S PERSPECTIVE: COMMON FEELINGS TEACHERS BRING TO A CONFERENCE

Many parents would be surprised to learn that conferences with parents are stressful and difficult for teachers. Like the parents, teachers too may feel that they are being judged and evaluated. They frequently find themselves in the position of presenting negative information or introducing problems to the parents, a role which is awkward and uncomfortable by nature. In fact, the underlying feelings that teachers bring to parent meetings are quite similar to those experienced by parents. For parents, understanding the teacher's perspective provides the foundation for developing a productive parent-teacher relationship. We will review five common feelings, which teachers bring to parent-teacher conferences:

1. *Fear:* "They'll decide 'I'm not a good teacher.'" Teachers are aware that many parents have had some exposure to different teaching styles than they have. They may fear that, in the parents' eyes, they will compare unfavorably against this child's other teachers. In today's schools, teachers often are asked to deal with needs of special education students, severe behavior problems, and other situations for which they feel underequipped and without the assistance they really need. They may be concerned that parents will pick up on their uncertainties and actually challenge their competence.

2. *Fear:* "They'll blame me for their child's problem." Related to the anxieties about being judged is the fear that parents will define their child's problem in terms of poor teaching methods or poor classroom management on the part of the teacher. While it is certainly possible that a teacher's approach or style is contributing to a child's difficulties, sometimes blaming or accusing a teacher provides a way for parents to cope with their feelings about the child's problem. All teachers sooner or later are victims of such accusations. A parent's self-confidence, openness, and understanding of teacher's reactions will greatly affect the teacher's level of defensiveness in parent-teacher conferences.

3. *Guilt:* "I shouldn't have waited so long to get to know these parents. We should have talked *before* there was a problem." As mentioned earlier, teachers often do not get to know the parents of all the children in their classroom, not due to lack of concern but rather to lack of time. This results all too frequently in a situation that is awkward for both teacher and parent—the communication of less than positive news to parents by someone who is essentially a stranger. While most teachers are aware of the importance of developing a good relationship with parents, they find this a difficult task to accomplish due to the everyday demands and pressures of their jobs. These guilt feelings may heighten the teacher's discomfort in discussing concerns with parents.

4. *Fear:* "They'll expect me to have answers I just don't have." While the teacher may be comfortable describing *what* the child's strengths, weaknesses or difficulties might be, parents often want to know *why* the child is having these difficulties. Teachers frequently are unprepared to answer such questions without additional professional input. In addition, parents may want to know about their child's future—about how a particular problem will affect the goals they and/or their child may have set. Sometimes the most honest answer to these questions is "I don't know," but this may be a difficult answer for a teacher to give parents. Sometimes this is due to the teacher's own expectations that s/he *should* know the answers; in other situations the parents incorrectly assume that the teacher *should* know the answers. The result in both cases is a lack of open communications.

5. *Guilt:* "With all the problems in my classroom, I'm too rushed to give anyone the attention they really need." Teachers are painfully aware of the lack of adequate resources in today's financially strained schools. They realize that the individual needs of some children may not be met fully in such a situation. Given the fact that the schools are legally responsible for meeting the educational needs of all children, the

teacher is constantly faced with doing what may be impossible. When faced with the parents of one specific child, the pressures and problems of insufficient resources are felt most acutely by the teacher. The conflicts inherent in this situation are particularly difficult to communicate to parents, who may sense the teacher's discomfort but remain unaware of its source.

COMMON DEFENSES USED BY PARENTS

Because feelings of guilt, fear and anxiety are difficult to express directly, people commonly resort to thoughts and behaviors which help them conceal these feelings from the awareness of others and themselves. Such thoughts and behaviors have been termed "defenses" and are a normal part of human communication patterns. While certain defenses may help people cope with difficult situations, they also may be obstacles to productive communication in other situations. We will review four of the specific defenses. used by some parents in dealing with teachers. These include:

1. *Blaming* the school or the teacher for the child's problems, e.g., "If he didn't have *that* teacher he's be fine." Blame, even if accurately placed, doesn't lead to improvements in most situations.

2. *Denying* that a problem exists, e.g., "I don't know what you're talking about. She behaves perfectly at home. It must be the *other* children." It is important for us to remember that children often exhibit different behaviors at home and at school due to the differences in the environments and in the tasks required of children. If a child's behavior at school is a problem, the parent's awareness and involvement is a very important part in finding a successful solution.

3. *Over-cooperating* or agreeing with anything the teacher says, even if you really disagree: "You're her teacher—you must be right!" In fact, it is quite possible for a teacher to make an error in judgment or interpretation regarding a specific child's needs. A parent may have a different opinion based on knowledge of the child that is far more extensive than that of the teacher. If a parent is unwilling or afraid to speak up, the teacher cannot benefit from the parent's knowledge and ideas. While teachers are "experts" in understanding and dealing with children, parents are experts about their children and should view the conference as an opportunity to work together with the teacher to solve the problem.

4. *Avoiding* the school and the teacher by not responding to the teacher's request for a meeting, not going to school open houses, or not showing up for scheduled appointments. By using this type of defense, the parent doesn't know what is happening to the child in school, and the school is unable to proceed with a formal evaluation of the child's needs. Finally, the fears and tensions created by active avoidance are generally far worse than the issues dealt with in a parent-teacher conference.

THE TEACHER'S PERSPECTIVE: COMMON DEFENSES USED

Needless to say, teachers are human and also use defenses to deal with uncomfortable feelings. Typical defensive behaviors engaged in by teachers include (a) *talking too fast* or too much, so that the parent can hardly get a word in; (b) *using professional jargon* that the parent does not understand, and (c) mentioning only positive things and *avoiding the negative;* (d) the importance of mentioning these behaviors is to point out to parents that teachers bring to a conference many of the same feelings as parents. Understanding their shared feelings and reactions can help both parents and teachers develop more open, direct communications which in turn will lead to more productive use of conference time for both.

PRACTICAL SUGGESTIONS FOR PARENTS: MAKING A CONFERENCE MORE PRODUCTIVE

1. Remember that the focus of the conference, and the common goal which you and the teacher share, is the best interest of your child, *not* your abilities as a parent.

2. Take some time before the conference to set your own goals for the conference. Even if the conference was requested by the teacher, it may be a good opportunity to answer questions you have or to find out more about your child's school experience.

3. Remember that asking questions about something you don't understand is a sign of interest and concern. School personnel may forget that certain terms which are familiar to them are unfamiliar to parents. Speaking up when you don't understand what is being said is most important. Without speaking up, you may not get the best understanding and all of the information from the conference which you wanted.

4. Try to separate the *information* being given from your reactions to that information. Make sure you are hearing the information accurately. One way of checking for accuracy is to repeat the points in your own words, e.g. "Let me see if I understand you correctly. You said that . . . ." While you will naturally have feelings about the information being shared, if you are not aware of these feelings, they may actually distort the information. This can lead to misunderstanding and wasted energy.

5. If you sense that the teacher is having difficulty sharing negative information, you can be helpful by saying that you are interested in both positive *and* negative feedback about your child. By communicating that you can handle negative information, you will help the teacher feel free enough to present a more accurate picture of your child's performance.

DATE DUE

MAY 0 6 1992			
DEC 0 7 1992			
DEC 0 2 1993			
AUG 0 6 1995			
DEC 1 2 1995			
MAR 0 7 1996			
JUN 2 3 1997			
AUG 2 1 1998			
SEP 0 9 2004			
SEP 2 3 2004			
MAR 1 7 2005			
DEC 2 2 2005			
AUG 1 8 2006			

DEMCO 38-297